Fifty Days On Board
A Slave - Vessel

Fifty Days On Board A Slave - Vessel

In the Mozambique Channel
April and May, 1843

Pascoe Grenfell Hill

Black Classic Press

Fifty Days On Board A Slave - Vessel

First published, 1848
Published by
Black Classic Press, 1993
All rights reserved
ISBN 0-933121-46-6
Cover art and design by Carles Juzang

Publication of *Fifty Days On Board A Slave - Vessel* was made possible through the cooperation of Kinya Kiongozi of Pyramid Press, Baltimore, MD. We are indebted to Mr. Kiongozi for bringing this rare volume to our attention and for providing his copy for use in the production of this book.

Printed on acid free paper to assure long life

Founded in 1978, Black Classic Press specializes in bringing to light obscure and significant works by and about people of African descent. If our books are not available in your area, ask your local bookseller to order them. Our current list of titles can be obtained by writing:

Black Classic Press
c/o List
P.O. Box 13414
Baltimore, MD 21203-3414

A Young Press With Some Very Old Ideas

TO

THE LORD ASHLEY, M.P.

My Lord,

I beg to inscribe the following pages to your Lordship, in the belief that, however defective as a literary production, consisting chiefly of Notes hastily penned on the deck of a Slave-vessel, they may present some claim to attention in the correctness and fidelity of their details.

I have the honour to be,

My Lord,

Your Lordship's most obedient

Humble Servant,

PASCOE GRENFELL HILL.

Cape of Good Hope,
September, 3, 1843.

CONTENTS.

FIFTY DAYS ON BOARD A SLAVE VESSEL. By the Rev. Pascoe Grenfell Hill, M.A., Chaplain of H.M.S. Cleopatra. Demy 12mo.

" We are all aware of the contents of a work which has been published within the last year, from the pen of a Chaplain on board one of the vessels employed on the African coast. In it the ruinous consequences of the policy which we have been so long following, are forcibly pointed out, while it has not, in the author's opinion, in any degree diminished the extent of the slave-trade, but has, on the contrary, greatly aggravated its horrors. Under these circumstances, I do think that we ought seriously to consider whether this is a policy in which we ought to persevere."—*Lord Howick on the Slave Trade.*

" What a scene of horror then ensues, I will not attempt to describe. Those who wish to judge of it may refer to the Rev. Mr. Hill's ' Fifty Days in a Slaver,' in which a calamity of this kind is recorded."—*Lord Palmerston on the Slave Trade.*

" In many cases their sufferings were aggravated to a degree which human imagination could hardly have conceived, if it had not become history in the narrative of ' Fifty Days on Board a Slaver,' published by the Rev. Pascoe Hill. The horrors described in that work, the perfect accuracy of which was guaranteed by the character of that gentleman, exceeded greatly any thing, he believed, which appeared at the time when almost every heart in England,—he wished for the sake of England he could say every heart,—was desirous of abolishing the trade itself."—*Sir R. H. Inglis on the Slave Trade.*

" This curious and succinct narrative gives the experience of a short voyage on board one of the Slave ships. We shall be rejoiced, if the publicity given to this little but intelligent work by our means, assist in drawing the attention of the influential classes to the subject."—*Blackwood's Magazine.*

" We hope this little book will have a wide circulation. We can conceive nothing so likely to do good to the righteous cause it is intended to promote."—*Examiner.*

" Mr. Hill is a pleasant, unaffected, and elegant writer, with a fund of good sense, and his brief and popular work is well adapted for general circulation."—*Spectator.*

" Will, if extensively read and pondered in a spirit of common, not to say Christian humanity, do more good in the way of practical results, towards the suppression of the Slave Trade, than fifty meetings at Exeter Hall."—*New Monthly Magazine.*

FIFTY DAYS ON BOARD A SLAVE VESSEL.

H. M. S. "CLEOPATRA," of twenty-six guns, commissioned by Capt. C. Wyvill, in April, 1842, having received orders to proceed to the Cape of Good Hope station, and to convey Lieut.-General Sir William Gomm to Mauritius, of which Island Sir William had been recently appointed Governor, sailed from Spithead in the latter part of July, and arrived at Rio Janeiro on the 6th of September. I was then in the "Malabar," of seventy-four guns, Capt. Sir George Sartorius, lying at Rio, and took advantage of the opportunity which the kindness of Commodore Purvis, senior officer on the station, afforded me, of getting transferred from that ship to the "Cleopatra."

The unrivalled magnificence of Rio harbour, narrow at the entrance, but spreading into a circumference of seventeen leagues; its hundred islands; the mountains which enclose it, showing every change of outline, covered with the richest verdure from the shore to their summits; the higher mountains beyond, which bound the view, mingling their heads with the clouds; compose a scene of variety and beauty which can hardly tire the eye. The city, on the left hand at the entrance, is four or five miles from the mouth of the harbour; the intermediate coast divided into several small bays, studded with pretty villages and country seats. These are still more numerous on the Braganza side of the harbour, opposite to Rio, the favourite resort

B

of its inhabitants during the heats of summer; a steam-
boat crossing hourly through the day. The scenery on
that side is not equally grand in character, but has more
softness, and the contrast is as great of its quiet and retire-
ment to the noise and bustle of the city. The usual land-
ing-place at Rio, is in front of the "Hotel Pharoux," a
very large and handsome building, which overlooks the
quay, the market, and the great square. In the square,
the principal objects are, the Palace of the Emperor, a
Carmelite convent, now applied to secular purposes, and
the Chapel Royal, adjacent to it. The busy stir on the
quay, of boats landing passengers, or taking off supplies to
the shipping; the still more busy and crowded market,
with its tropical profusion of fruits and vegetables; above
all, the different tribes of the human race, of every hue
and feature, who throng it; offer a curious and lively scene.
The proportion of the coloured population to the white, in
the province of Rio Janeiro generally, is probably not less
than twenty to one. On the plantations in the interior,
where this proportion is greatest, the sufferings of the
negroes are doubtless severest. In the metropolis, their
condition does not wear that mournful appearance in which
the imagination is apt to present it. Certainly the con-
tent and cheerfulness of the motley crowd here seems to
equal that of the common classes in most other countries.
The heartiest mirth prevails among the parties who mingle
around the small charcoal fires on which they fry their
fish, or boil their cassava root and sweet potato. The
hardest labour witnessed in the streets, is that of the coffee-
carriers, who bear bags of great weight on their heads, at
a running pace, to the sound of some rattling substances
in a bladder, which the leader of the party shakes, and
the others accompany with their voices. The number of
hours for which this toil is exacted from them on their
masters' account, still leaves them a portion of the day to
work for their own profit, permitting them, by industry,

within a reasonable time, to purchase their freedom. And it is to the credit of the Brazilians, that the moment which releases the negro from slavery, raises him wholly above the contempt and ignominy to which his race is subject in some other slave countries, on account of colour. The situation of the domestic slaves in Brazil is more favourable than that of any others. But although cases of cruelty towards them do not often come into notice, there is no doubt that they are frequently over-worked, under-fed, and otherwise harshly treated, dependent on the caprice of an ill-tempered or avaricious owner. Even the more humane insist that it is impossible to get their negroes to work without the use of the rod. "Il faut les frapper," remarked a French lady to me. A flogging can be legally inflicted only by sentence of a magistrate, whose award is generally one of extreme severity.

I attended one of the slave-auctions which take place usually every week, having been previously advertised in the Gazettes. About twenty-five of both sexes, decently dressed, were seated on benches behind a long table, which as each in turn ascended to be better viewed by the bidders, a sullenness of look seemed to express their feeling of degradation in being thus put up to sale. The prices seldom rose above 300 mil-reis, about £31; but it is to be supposed that those who are thus disposed of by auction are among the least useful or valuable to their owners. It is not uncommon to meet negroes in the streets, moving slowly with shackled feet, or with a heavy iron collar round the neck, usually denoting a recovered fugitive. Advertisements of runaway negroes often fill a column in the daily journals. In one of these, taken up at hazard, " Jornal do Comercio, 13 de Agosto de 1842," I find the following:—

" Disappeared, on the 16th inst., from Rua do Cano, N. 2, a negro boatman, named Sebastian, native of Inhambane : rather full-bodied, of ordinary height, dressed in a dirty white shirt and trowsers, and accompanied by a black dog, answering to the name of 'Cara-linda.' Whoever may apprehend and take him to the House of Correction, and give information thereof at the above address, will be rewarded for his trouble."

" Ran away, on the 8th inst., at eight in the morning, from Dr. Jose Julio de Freitas Continho, N. 106, Rua do Hospicio, a negro woman, his slave, named Maria, native of Congo, about twenty-five years of age, of a deeper black than usual, well-made in person, countenance handsome; teeth white and regular; bearing marks on her arms, and one, by incision, on her hand; drest in a dark gown, with striped handkerchief, and red glass-earrings. She has taken with her two white gowns, shoes, socks, a lace shawl, a petticoat of stout calico, and a shift of the same. It is supposed that she has been decoyed away and kept in concealment. Whoever may detain her is hereby protested against; and any one who may discover and bring her to the above house will be suitably rewarded."

" Ran away, the 31st ult., a black, named Pedro, native of Mozambique, wearing a cotton shirt and trowsers, and an iron round his neck,"—&c.

" Whoever may apprehend and bring to N. 112, Rua de San Pedro, an old black woman, named Eva, who has run away, drest in a dark striped gown, carrying with her a case of sweetmeats, a box of linen, several pairs of shoes (being a great thief,) and having one of her eyes closed up, will be well rewardeed."

" Ran away, on the 12th inst., at one in the afternoon, a moleque (young male slave,) named José, drest in a striped cotton shirt and trowsers, somewhat dirty from use in the kitchen,"—&c.

" Ran away from the Caminho das Larangeiras, a black, named Bento, of ordinary stature, having a wound on one of his cheek-bones: drest in a white shirt and trowsers,"— &c.

Parallel to the Marinha or water-side, is the Rua Direita,

the widest street in Rio, which it traverses in its whole breadth ; the other principal streets going off at right angles from it, through the length of the city. Of these, the first in attraction is the Rua Ouvidor, containing the most showy shops, chiefly French, and several circulating libraries, stocked with modern French literature. Towards the upper part of the harbour, the Rua Direita terminates in the ascent to a hill, on which is situated the spacious Benedictine convent, still tenanted by some monks of that order. It has fared better with this than with many other ecclesiastical edifices, as witnessed in the roofless walls of the Jesuits' College, occupying a somewhat similar hill in the part of the town towards the harbour's mouth. One may regard, in the Southern Hemisphere, the ruins which mark the downfall of that Order, with feelings different from those which such a spectacle would excite in Europe, recalling to mind the brave and unwearied opposition made by its members to the iniquitous slave-traffic of their countrymen in Brazil. The Carmelite convent, in the great square already mentioned, about midway between the Jesuits' and the Benedictine, has met a sort of middle fate, it being appropriated to secular uses. [Within its precincts, is the Royal Library, brought from Portugal by King John VI., in 1808, consisting of nearly 10,000 volumes, containing many Portuguese and French Theological and historical works. Among the few English books, I found Southey's " History of Brazil," and in its pages the following passages :—" Europe had no cause to rejoice in the establishment of the Jesuits ; but in Brazil and Paraguay their superstition may be forgiven them for the noble efforts which they made in behalf of the oppressed Indians."—Vol. ii. 232.

" The Jesuits opposed the Indian slave-trade with the zeal of men who knew that they were doing their duty : never had men a better cause, and never did men engage in any cause with more heroic ardour."—*Ib.* 308.

The " Cleopatra," after a week's stay at Rio, sailed on the 14th of September for the Cape of Good Hope, and arrived in sight of it on Sunday, the 9th of October. After repeated endeavours, against a strong south-easter, to weather the Cape, in order to get round to Simon's Bay, the usual anchorage for our ships of war, on Wednesday morning, the sea running very high, and the wind showing no disposition to abatement or change, it was found advisable to bear up for Table Bay, on the west side of the Cape, where we anchored the same afternoon. The approach to the " Cape of Storms" is often a subject of anxiety to the navigator; but to the passenger, weary of a long voyage, no place can afford a more pleasant relief than Cape Town. It has broad, handsome streets, shaded by trees; well-furnished shops; excellent roads in its vicinity; and a most delightful and healthy climate. On my way overland, to meet the " Cleopatra" at Simon's Bay, I spent a few days at the village of Wynberg, near Constantia, in a scene of complete rural quiet and beauty.

We sailed from Simon's Bay at the end of October, and arrived about the middle of the following month at Port Louis, Mauritius. Sir William Gomm, whose reputation had preceded him thither, was welcomed with acclamation to his new Government ; and we had much to regret in the loss of his society, and that of Lady Gomm, to which their fellow-voyagers in the " Cleopatra" remain indebted for many agreeable hours. I felt a desire to trace the scenery in this island so minutely described in the elegant fiction of St. Pierre. Taking the book in my hand, and carefully marking every indication which it afforded, I bent my steps towards the " Embrasure," in the mountain-ridge behind Port Louis,—" cette ouverture escarpée au haut de la montagne"—near which the author fixes the residence of " Paul et Virginie." After various ineffectual attempts to cross the mountain in that direction, I at length took the road to Pamplemousses—" le chemin qui mène du Port

Louis au quartier des Pamplemousses,"—after proceeding on which two or three miles, a turning leads round to the back of the mountain, where nothing appears but its black, perpendicular side, of immense height, and a long, rough slope, which ascends to it from the plain. I made my way, however, up this ascent; and at the foot of the precipice, completely overshadowed by it, suddenly opened before me the "bassin," the spot of which I was in search. I entered a labyrinth of trees and flowering shrubs; the fragrant yellow acacia (Arabica,) the goyava in fruit; and other kinds, which I had not seen common elsewhere. There were, indeed, no traces of human habitation, except remains of former enclosures, which showed that the place had not been always lonely and neglected. Birds, roused by my entrance, flew from tree to tree, mingling their various notes on all sides; the only sounds which broke on the deep solitude. The path thence to Port Louis, through an opening in the intervening ridge, commands a view of the church of Pamplemousses, of the "Trois Mamelles," and, at the same time, of the harbour and Signal-hill;—"le Morne de la Découverte, avec la mer au loin, où apparaissait quelquefois un vaisseau qui venait de l'Europe, ou qui y retournait;"—exactly corresponding to the view described by St. Pierre, and, indeed, beyond a doubt, taken by him on this very spot.

At the beginning of December, the "Cleopatra," quitted Mauritius, to proceed round the north point of Madagascar, to her appointed cruizing ground, in the Mozambique Channel. A new interest here attached itself to every sail which came in sight. The slave-trade on the east coast of Africa is at present almost confined to the districts of Quilimane and Sofala, having ceased at the port of Mozambique, through the zealous exertions of its late and present Governors. This zeal on their part has been attributed to the increase made of late years in the legal emoluments of the Government; the smallness of which, formerly, admitted temptation to add to them by patronising the exportation of slaves. The City of Mozambique occupies an island across the middle of the harbour, about a mile and a quarter in length,—scarcely a quarter of a mile in its greatest breadth. At one extremity is a very strong, handsome fort, built at the commencement of the sixteenth century. The island is low and sandy, with little vegetation except a few sickly palms, and depends for supplies on the adjacent coast. The present population is about 3,000, consisting chiefly of negro slaves, with a mixture of Malays, Johannians, Hindoo bunneahs, or traders, and a few Portuguese creoles. I met in the streets a much greater proportion of shackled slaves than at Rio Janeiro. The negroes inhabit cane huts, along the beach, and on the outskirts of the town ; and I was struck with the order and decorum which prevailed among them. On remarking this to a Portuguese, named Nobre, the owner of the only large store in the place, he said—" Better for them, else their backs would smart." He candidly expressed his hatred to the English, for their exertions to suppress the slave-trade.

We crossed the channel, in the beginning of January, 1843, from the African shore, to the Bay of St. Augustine, on the coast of Madagascar, for the purpose of taking in fresh provisions and water. A small merchant schooner, from Mauritius, lay there at anchor on our arrival, surrounded by about twenty canoes, full of natives, who immediately paddled towards our ship. As they approached, a multitude of voices, vying with each other, proclaimed the names and titles of our visitors. " Me broder Prince Will," meaning, I believe, " Prince of Wales ;" " Me John Green ;" " Me Dungaree ;" " Me Jem Bravo ;" " You my very good friend,—me come aboard, speaky the captain." They appeared to me a very fine race of savages ; their dark-brown skins sleek and glossy ; their well-formed limbs supple from continual exertion ; all their actions and gestures free and agile. Their features are far from disagreeable, with an intelligent, vivacious expression ; their jet-black hair plaited with great care and cleanliness, and by no means untastefully. The canoes, which held about four each, were twenty feet in length, very narrow, and sharp at both ends. Though frail in appearance, being formed of the soft " cabbage wood," they are, in reality, safe, two long transverse poles suspending a solid piece of the same light wood, which, floating on the water, balances the canoe, and precludes the possibility of its upsetting. Most of our visitors were nearly naked, except a few whom the pride of distinction had led to disguise their persons in an old naval coat or cap, sometimes with the addition of a cast off épaulette, and a profusion of brass nails or buttons. On being admitted on board the ship, their volubility increased, having at command a great number of English words, many of which they pronounce with great clearness, unfettered, it may be supposed, by any grammatical connection. One, who announced himself as " Captain Long," addressed me in the most earnest tone of supplication :—

" Look here,—you very good friend to me : I love you very well ; all de same one fader ; you speaky the captain."

" What shall I say for you to the captain ?"

" You speaky for me ; he give me one cape" (cap).

This petitioner had two brothers, bearing the same family name, but distinguished as " Young Long," and " Jem Long." These, though not above begging, deemed it beneath their dignity to bring shells for sale.

" No,—no get shell ; me big man : sing out, ' Fellow, go get shell !'—me have bullock,—speaky the king, Prince Will."

Several brought their assagais, or long spears, which they were not unwilling to barter for beads, buttons, or " clouty" (cotton cloth.)

In the afternoon, I landed at a village within the mouth of the river which empties itself into St. Augustine's Bay. The huts, about fifty in number, are neatly constructed of

clay and reed, but so low, that it would require one to stoop
double in order to enter the door. Here we found "Prince
Will," a dwarfish, most wretched object, in extreme old
age, one eye completely overspread by a hideous kind of
fungus. He was engaged at a sort of "palaver," on the
occasion of receiving some embassage from his brother
potentate, "King Voose," whose Government includes the
territory on the other side of the river. Their titles are
apparently hereditary, and their authority, I believe, sub-
ordinate to that of "King Baba," who resides at some
distance in the interior. "Prince Will" was seated on the
ground, under the shade of some fine trees, amid a circle of
above a hundred warlike-looking men, also seated on their
haunches, some having muskets, and all holding long spears
erect in their hands. He seemed entirely engrossed in
smoking his pipe, and incapable of taking any interest in
the business going forward, which was conducted on his
part by three or four who sat near him. All preserved
great gravity of demeanour, and took not the slightest
notice of our presence. Many women and children, who
had attended us from our landing, kept back at a respectful
distance while we approached the circle, but again thronged
us after we withdrew from it, on our return to the boat.
Some of them were even pressing to enter it, and accompany us on board. One asked : "King ship take queeny ?
Queeny come aboard ?" The title "Queeny" is given to
their women, generally. On being told that their wish
could not be complied with, they signified their discontent
very strongly. The shameless licentiousness of the women,
encouraged and promoted by their men, appears almost
universal.

On the morning after our arrival, "Prince Will,"—notice
having been duly sent of his intention,—paid us a visit on
board, bringing with him a large train of attendants.
Captain Wyvill having put in requisition all the chairs
which could be got, his cabin was soon completely filled,

and we were not then left long in suspense as to the purport of the visit. A young man stood forward, and delivered, with much gesticulation, a somewhat disjointed harangue, the object of which, however, was sufficiently obvious. " Prince Will very good friend to you, you very good friend Prince Will ; you come here catch water, catch bullock,—very good. Prince Will, him no got powder, no got clouty,—Prince Will, him drink brandy ?"

Our decks were crowded, on this and following days, with natives, bringing shells for sale—harps, cowries, volutes, and others, in great variety ; also a few water-melons and pumpkins. One " Captain Harribee," from Tullear Bay, about ten miles distant, objected to barter : " No sell, give ;" he asked for a bottle and some " clouty," and afterwards sent us a present of a fowl and a basket of eggs. Another man, who had received a Spanish dollar for two assagais, was asked what use he would make of the money ? " Get ten dollar, buy slave. Got one, two, three slave,—bring water, bring wood." Most of our visitors wear, around the neck, attached to a string of beads, among shells and other ornaments, a small piece of leather, which they call " Mahommed;" and believe has a charm to protect from death. " Where," I asked one of them, " do we go when we die ?" " You die, takee shore,—Tent-Rock, oder place, —put in ground." " And never get up again ?" " No, no get up." "But you must die too." " No, I no die." Jem Long, to whom I put the question, " Do you ever pray to God ?" answered, " Malgash no see God ; what for pray ?" The captain of the Mauritius schooner, a Frenchman, taking in here a cargo of *orseille*, a species of lichen, which produces a fine dye, tells me that the natives in this part of the island belong to the tribe called " Secalaves." He mentions also the " Baignemasaques," " Antolôtes," and other Frenchified names. The main distinction, however, is between these tribes, who inhabit most of the west coast, and the Oovahs, occupying the north part of the island

and the whole of its east coast, who own the sovereignty of the Queen of Madagascar, and are much more advanced towards civilisation.

From St. Augustine's Bay, the "Cleopatra" proceeded to Algoa Bay, in the Cape of Good Hope colony, the south limit of our cruising station. This port alone has easy communication with the productive districts in the interior of the colony. Its principal exports during the year 1842 were :—

Wool	.	. value £43,560	Tallow	.	. value £2,899
Ox and horse hides		19,494	Horns	.	. . 1,066
Goat skins	.	. 9,503	Aloes	.	. . 5,644
Butter	.	. 2,907	Ivory	.	. . 1,964

The town, Port Elizabeth, contains upwards of 3000 British inhabitants, and increases rapidly in population and importance. We found here nine English merchant-vessels at anchor. I made a visit to Uitenhage, about twenty miles distant, chief town of the division of the same name, to which Port Elizabeth belongs. It is pleasantly situated in a fertile valley, sheltered by a low range of hills, and watered by the Zwartkop river. Every house has its enclosures of peach, apple, or pear trees; giving the whole an appearance of one large garden. The population is about 2000, half of the number coloured. The remainder chiefly Dutch, the English not amounting to one hundred. The time of the criminal sessions was approaching, and the municipal authorities of Uitenhage were making preparation for the visit of the judges in circuit. Mr. Brunett, clerk of the peace, informed me, that since the abolition of slavery the average quarterly number of criminal cases for trial in this division, containing 9000 square miles, and 11,000 inhabitants, had diminished from 25 to 4. It is only to be regretted that the measure of slave-emancipation was not carried into effect in this colony with more consideration for its peculiar circumstances. The compensation awarded to the slave-owners here, through misunderstanding on the part of the Boers, or their inability to wait till the time appointed for its payment, fell, in a great measure, into the hands of brokers at Cape Town, who purchased their claims at a very low rate. The dissatisfaction and distrust occasioned by this measure have been the cause of the rebellious disturbances which have arisen in the colony during the last five years, and which are now at a higher pitch than ever. Mr. Brunett expressed to me the anxious desire of the English inhabitants to obtain a resident clergyman at Uitenhage ; and showed me a good house and garden provided by them for a lay catechist, or schoolmaster, who had just left them, which they would gladly settle on a clergyman of the Church of England, who should come among them, as well as contribute, in a reasonable degree, to his support. I remember that Mr. Dickenson, clerk of the peace at Stellenbosch, twenty-five miles from Cape Town, held nearly similar language. That gentleman regretted to me that, instead of a schoolmaster sent by Government, at a salary of £230 per annum, who exercised the Hottentots in questions concerning " oxygen, hydrogen, latent caloric," &c., a clergyman had not been sent to administer the ordinances of the Church, as well as give due attention to the education of the poor. It is the painful truth that, in this vast colony, though thirty-seven years have elapsed since it passed into the hands of the English, the Church of England is still *unrepresented*.

The " Cleopatra," on her return to the north, cruised along the African coast, and anchored ten miles off the bar of Quilimane, arly in February. Shortly after, I accompanied a party, in one of our boats, to the town, situated about eight miles up the river, on its left bank. The water on the bar, at the time of our crossing it, was quite smooth ; but even a moderate breeze will curl the sea, to a great extent around, into formidable breaking waves. The sides of the river on each hand are a thicket of mangroves. Several recesses in these, sheltered large flat-bottomed boats,

which are used to carry negroes to the slave-vessels outside
the bar. Pelicans, curlews, and other water-birds flew
around us. At two places, several hippopotami raised their
heads above the surface, resembling, with their curved
tusks, the twisted stumps of large trees. On a ball being
fired at them, snorting up the water from their nostrils,
they plunged beneath it. I longed to see one of the mon-
sters in its full proportions, when, looking on a small island,
"Pequena Banca," just in the mid river, about 150 yards
distant, appeared one standing on dry ground. The animal
perceived us as soon, and ran to and fro with a speed hardly
to be expected from its unwieldy bulk ; sometimes stopping
to take a look at us, as if doubting which way to go, and,
entering the water, gradually disappeared, not before I had
sent a bullet at it, which, however, had no chance of pene-
trating its thick, tough hide. In size it approached the
elephant : but the shortness of its legs gave it rather th
figure of the pig. We were most hospitably received at Quilimane, by Senhor Azevedo, a rich Portuguese gentleman,
who carries on a considerable commerce in ivory and gold-
dust. The exportation of slaves he professed to hold in
abomination, and is at variance on that point with the present Governor of the district of Quilimane, whom he repre-
sents as conniving at it. Azevedo assured us he had certain
intelligence that, during this and the following month,
four to six slave-vessels may be confidently expected at
this port. The European inhabitants of Quilimane do not
exceed ninety souls. The principal houses are well built,
with extensive walled premises. Rice-grounds occupy a
swamp in the midst of the population, in which are the
numerous mud huts of the negro slaves. I thought the
rice of sweeter flavour than even the Egyptian. No more,
however, is grown than is sufficient for the consumption of
the inhabitants. The prevalence of the slave-trade here
has had its usual effect in damping all other spirit of enterprise. The handsomest feature of the place is a large

grove of lofty cocoa-nut palms, which afford a delicious shade. The mangoes are good, though inferior to those of Mauritius ; the plantains dry and flavourless.

About the middle of February, the " Cleopatra" proceeded from Quilimane to recruit her stock of water at St. Augustine's Bay. Our return thither was hailed, shortly after our arrival, by "Jem Bravo," "Young Long," and others of our former acquaintance. Disgust, however, at their endeavour to impose on us, by asking ten dollars each for bullocks, small and lean, the fair price for which would have been three or four dollars per head, hastened our departure, as soon as the business of watering was completed. On March 2nd, having gone away in a boat to a neighbouring reef, on a shelling excursion, while returning to the ship after dark, I perceived in the west horizon a remarkable column of light, resembling a radiation. Two or three days subsequently, the whole being visible above the horizon at sunset, it became evident that it was a distinct celestial body ; a comet, with a tail, on a rough measurement, of about forty degrees in length, travelling in at northerly and westerly direction.

On March 4th, we left St. Augustine's Bay for Port Natal, desirous to learn how affairs went on there, previous to our return to Quilimane ; and anchored off Natal Bar on Sunday, March 12th. On the following morning, I crossed the bar in one of our cutters, which, the evening before, had been nearly swamped on it, and lost two of her oars. Lieut. Nourse, in command of the " Fawn" schooner, at anchor inside the harbour, told me that, from an account kept by him during a year, it resulted that there are, on an average, twelve days only in each month on which the bar is passable. There are about 200 soldiers here at present, under command of Major Smith—part at the " Point," just within the harbour's mouth, where a small fort is erected, and part at the Camp, two miles distant, on the site where the same officer, with a force of 100 men, withstood a siege of the

Boers. The existing relation between the British troops and the insurgents is that of a suspension of hostilities, without any acknowledgment yet made by the Boers of the sovereignty of England.

The " Cleopatra" re-anchored off the bar of Quilimane on the 23rd of March, and, the same day, sent the barge up the river to the town.

March 26th.—The barge, which was dispatched to Quilimane, returned this morning, with the news that H. M. brig " Lily" had, during our absence, driven a slave-vessel ashore, and carried off two others, barques, prizes to the Cape; bringing, also, a letter from the Governor of " Quilimane and Rios de Senna," in a far from congratulatory tone on the subject. His version of the affair stated that, on the 4th of this month, the Portuguese brig of war, " Gentil Libertador," crossing the bar of the river at daybreak, perceived a vessel approaching the shore, which the " Lily," then anchored outside, perceiving at the same moment, immediately weighed anchor. The vessel in question, judging it impossible to escape, continued her course to the shore, where she grounded at half-past seven, about six miles from the port. A quarter of an hour after, the Portuguese brig took possession of the stranded vessel, and hoisted on board of her the Portuguese flag. The Governor complains of the " Lily's" boats having afterwards forcibly boarded the prize, and destroyed various parts of the vessel. We have grounds for more than suspicion that, had not an English cruiser been on the coast, the " Gentil Libertador" would not have interfered with the proceedings of the slave vessel. The Governor's despatch proceeds to state, that, on the 20th of this month, the crews of the two Brazilian barques, " Desengaño," and " Confidencia," captured by H. M. brig " Lily," presented themselves before him, part having been put ashore, and part on board the boat of the pilot belonging to this port, at that time on service at the bar; and expatiates on the peril of their being thus let loose on a country far from all inhabitants, except those of the town, exposed to the risk of being devoured by wild beasts.

Friday, March 31st.—A sail was observed this morning, apparently a brigantine, stealing along shore to the south of the Quilimane river. At noon, the weather being calm, I took a seat in the barge, which, with the pinnace, were ordered away, manned and armed, to overhaul the vessel, or failing in that, to proceed up the river to Quilimane. Soon after leaving the ship, a light breeze sprung up, and the boats made sail. After steering a good while in the direction in which the vessel had been seen from the ship, we unexpectedly caught sight of her two or three points farther to windward than we had supposed her to be, and, to our surprise, standing towards the frigate, which lay at anchor. About the same time we perceived a boat pulling furiously in that direction, which proved to belong to the Portuguese brig of war, anchored inside the bar. It seemed doubtful which of us would win the race ; and we anxiously watched for some movement on the part of the " Cleopatra," who had now the breeze, as well as ourselves. At length we saw her, at the same moment, cross her royal yards, and make sail. On this, the brigantine, taking alarm, hauled her wind. The race, meanwhile, continued between our boats and the Portuguese, till one of their rowers, probably from a *coup-de-soleil*, was obliged to quit his oar, which made them drop astern. The night approaching, compelled our boats also to abandon the chase, and, having stood on the same course half an hour after it became dark, we turned our heads back in the direction of the Quilimane river. On our return, falling in with the " Cleopatra," who continued the pursuit, the officer in charge of the boats wished to communicate with her, and supposed that she had hove to, in order to enable him to do so. Incautiously approaching her head, when close to her bows, we found that she had been just in stays, and, not perceiving our boat in the darkness, had gathered way, and was coming right down on us. In vain we hailed : " Put your helm hard a-port." No answer was returned. There was no possibility of getting out of her way. " She is right into us." A few hands were near the bowsprit, to whom we cried : " Throw us plenty of ropes." I had hastily doffed my great coat, in readiness for a swim ; and, after an instant's hesitation whether it would be better to jump overboard, or await the shock, and the chance of catching a rope, found my hand close to the dolphin-striker, which I seized, and the next instant, clambering up I scarce knew how, clasped the image of Cleopatra, the figure-head of the frigate. Our boat had providentially been perceived just in time to throw all the sails of the frigate a-back, before the collision, which, otherwise, would have been inevitable destruction to most of us. Of those who remained in the boat, only one was disabled, no other injury being done to the barge than smashing her mainmast : I rejoined my comrades in her, and we proceeded towards the mouth of the river. Unable, however, from the darkness of the night to make sure of the entrance, we anchored outside the surf, and, the next morning, received a kind welcome from our hospitable friend Azevedo, at Quilimane. As we sat, after dinner, enjoying the cool of the evening, under a porch, he said to me, " Monsieur Hill, voulez-vous voir un Prince noir ?" On my assenting, he dispatched a request for the presence of the royal personage, who soon made his appearance, with a dozen attendants, from an adjacent house allotted for their use. This was a chief of the Macoa tribe, from about two hundred miles in the interior, who had brought some gold-dust and ivory for Azevedo. He and his train had very little clothing among them ; their arms and legs ornamented with rings of hippopotamus hide. Having been put in spirits by a distribution of brandy, they performed a dance, as void of grace and agility as all other negro-dances that I have seen ; accompanying the exhibition by clapping their hands, and a most discordant vocal chorus, the same, Azevedo told me, which they use when they go to hunt the hippopotamus, and well calculated to astound the animal, if that be their object. In return for this entertainment, two or three musical-boxes were set a-playing, with which the " Black Prince" was so much pleased, that he offered to give four of his attendants for one of them.

On the following day, we descended the river, and found the " Cleopatra" again anchored off its mouth, having failed in pursuit of the brigantine. The same afternoon we weighed anchor for the island of " Fogo," about 100 miles to the north, where slave-vessels frequently seek shelter; leaving the barge and a cutter to guard the entrance to the Quilimane river. Finding nothing at Fogo, the pinnace was sent to look into the small rivers along the shore to Mozambique, 100 miles further to the north, where she rejoined us after a fruitless search; and on Monday, April 10th, we began to retrace our course to the south.

Wednesday, April 12th.—At day-break this morning, being again off Fogo, on return to Quilimane, the look-out at the top mast-head perceived a vessel on the lee-quarter, at such a distance as to be scarcely visible; but, her locality being pronounced very suspicious, the order was given to " bear up for her." Our breeze was light, and, falling still lighter, at 9 A.M. the boats were ordered out, and, in a few minutes, the barge and the first gig, manned and armed, were pulling away in the direction of the stranger. So variable, however, is the weather at this season, that, before the boats had rowed a mile from the ship, a squall gathered on our beam, and a thick haze surrounded us, hiding the chase from sight: rain fell in torrents, and we were going seven knots through the water, not waiting to hoist in the barge. The fog clearing away, the sun broke forth, and the rakish-looking brigantine, as we now perceived her to be, appeared to have carried on all sail during the squall. A steady breeze succeeded, and we began to feel pretty confident as to the issue of the race. On mounting a few steps up the rigging, we could see, under her sails, the low, black hull, pitching up and down ; and, being now within range of our shot, one of the forecastle guns was cleared away for a bow-chaser. The British ensign had been for some time flying at our peak,—at length answered by the green and yellow Brazilian flag. Orders were given to "man the foremost quarters on the main-deck," and the due elevation given to the guns, when, suddenly, the brigantine dropt her peak, shortened sail, and rounded to, as to wait for our coming up. Her pursuer, in consequence, also shortened sail, immediately on which, she again made sail, and was off, in a different direction, across our bows. No time was lost in bracing our yards in pursuit, and sending back the hands to their quarters at the guns. As soon as it was brought to bear, the foremost gun was fired ; and after an eager watch of a few seconds, the ball ploughed the waters just across the bows of the chase. Another and another followed in quick succession, equally unregarded by the brigantine ; and fifteen to twenty shot were fired, some ahead, some astern, some over, till, as we were evidently gaining on her every minute, and the chance of escape became desperate, she at length shortened sail, and lay-to in good earnest. We now ranged up alongside, and eager eyes were turned on every part of the vessel. Dark, naked forms passing across her deck removed the least remaining doubt as to her character, and showed us that she had her human cargo aboard. A cutter being hoisted out, an officer was sent to take possession, and the British ensign displaced the Brazilian. Capt. Wyvill, whom I accompanied, then followed, taking with him the surgeon, to inspect the state of health on board the prize. It was a strange scene which presented itself to us when we mounted her side. The deck was crowded to the utmost with naked negroes, to the number, as stated in her papers, of 450, in almost riotous confusion, having revolted, before our arrival, against their late masters ; who, on their part, also showed strong excitement, from feelings, it may be supposed, of no pleasant nature. The negroes, a meagre, famished-looking throng, having broken through all control, had seized everything to which they had a fancy in the vessel ; some with hands full of "farinha," the powdered root of the mandioc or cassava ; others with large pieces of pork and beef, having broken open the casks ; and some had taken fowls from the coops, which they devoured raw. Many were busily dipping rags, fastened to bits of string, into the water-casks ; and, unhappily, there were some who, by a like method, got at the contents of a cask of "aguardiente," fiery Brazilian rum, of which they drank to excess. The addition of our boat's crews to this crowd left hardly room to move on the deck. The shrill hubbub of noises, which I cannot attempt to describe, expressive, however, of the wildest joy, thrilled on the ear, mingled with the clank of the iron, as they were knocking off their fetters on every side. It seemed that, from the moment the first ball was fired, they had been actively employed in thus freeing themselves, in which our men were not slow in lending their assistance. I counted but thirty shackled together in pairs ; but many more pairs of shackles were found below. We were not left an instant in doubt as to the light in which they viewed us. They crawled in crowds, and rubbed caressingly our feet and clothes with their hands, even rolling themselves, as far as room allowed, on the deck before us. And when they saw the crew of the vessel rather unceremoniously sent over the side into the boat which was to take them prisoners to the frigate, they sent up a long, universal shout of triumph and delight.

Account was now taken of the number of the negroes, amounting to 447. Of these were 189 men, few, however, if any, exceeding 20 years of age ; 45 women ; 213 boys. The number of sick among them was reckoned at 25.* Captain Wyvill proposed to take 100 on board the "Cleopatra." This humane and judicious intention was, however, unfortunately prevented from taking effect, owing to an erroneous impression that some of them were infected with the small-pox. Our prize proves to be the same vessel which we chased on the 31st ult., off Quilimane; her name, the "Progresso," last from Paranagua, in Brazil, and bound, as her crew state, to Rio Janeiro. They are seventeen in number, and, with a few exceptions, active-looking, able-bodied men : three Spaniards; the rest Portuguese, or Brazilians. They quitted the coast only last evening, and have thus been captured by us within a few hours after the embarkation of their cargo. The vessel is of about 140 tons; the length of the slave-deck, 37 feet; its mean breadth, 21½ feet; its height, 3½ feet. The captain, if we may credit the statement of the crew, was, with another man, drowned in the surf, where they embarked the negroes; and the absence of the long-boat gives some probability to the story. A Spaniard, of Barcelona, by name Antonio Vallel, replied to my inquiries, "No hay quien manda; tan capitanes somos uno como otro."—"There is no one who commands; we are captains as much one as another." This man, with another Spaniard, of Galicia, Sebastian Vicete, and a Portuguese, named Manoel, employed to cook for the negroes, were sent back into the prize. An interpreter being much wanted to communicate with them, concerning the care and management of the negroes, I offered my services during the voyage, to which Captain Wyvill having assented, at 7 o'clock in the evening I found myself, with my servant and carpet bag, on board the "Progresso," under sail for the Cape of Good Hope. The English previously sent on board were, the lieutenant in charge, a master's assistant, a quarter-master, a boatswain's mate, and nine seamen.

* This calculation was afterwards found to be much too low.

During the first watch, our breeze was light and variable, the water smooth, the recently liberated negroes sleeping, or lying in quietness about the deck. Their slender supple limbs entwine in a surprisingly small compass ; and they resembled, in the moonlight, confused piles of arms and legs, rather than distinct human forms. They were, however, apparently at ease, and all seemed going on as fairly as could be desired. But the scene was soon to undergo a great and terrible change. About one hour after midnight, the sky began to gather clouds, and a haze overspread the horizon to windward. A squall approached, of which I and others, who had lain down on the deck, received warning by a few heavy drops of rain. Then ensued a scene, the horrors of which it is impossible to depict. The hands having to shorten sail suddenly, uncertain as to the force of the squall, found the poor helpless creatures lying about the deck, an obstruction to getting at the ropes and doing what was required. This caused the order to send them all below, which was immediately obeyed. The night, however, being intensely hot and close, 400 wretched beings thus crammed into a hold 12 yards in length, 7 in breadth, and only $3\frac{1}{2}$ feet in height, speedily began to make an effort to reissue to the open air. Being thrust back, and striving the more to get out, the after-hatch was forced down on them. Over the other hatchway, in the fore-part of the vessel, a wooden grating was fastened. To this, the sole inlet for the air, the suffocating heat of the hold, and, perhaps, panic from the strangeness of their situation, made them press ; and thus great part of the space below was rendered useless. They crowded to the grating, and clinging to it for air, completely barred its entrance. They strove to force their way through apertures, in length 14 inches, and barely 6 inches in breadth, and, in some instances, succeeded. The cries, the heat,—I may say, without exaggeration, " the smoke of their torment,"—which ascended, can be compared to nothing earthly. One of the Spaniards

gave warning that the consequence would be "many deaths."
—" Mañana habrà muchos muertos."

Thursday, April 13th. (Passion Week).—The Spaniard's
prediction of last night, this morning was fearfully verified.
Fifty-four crushed and mangled corpses lifted up from the
slave-deck have been brought to the gang-way and thrown
overboard. Some were emaciated from disease; many,
bruised and bloody. Antonio tells me that some were found
strangled, their hands still grasping each other's throats,
and tongues protruding from their mouths. The bowels of
one were crushed out. They had been trampled to death
for the most part, the weaker under the feet of the stronger
in the madness and torment of suffocation from crowd and
heat. It was a horrid sight, as they passed one by one,—
the stiff distorted limbs smeared with blood and filth,—to
be cast into the sea. Some, still quivering, were laid on the
deck to die; salt water thrown on them to revive them,
and a little fresh water poured into their mouths. Antonio
reminded me of his last night's warning, " Ya se lo dixè
anoche." He actively employed himself, with his comrade
Sebastian, in attendance on the wretched living beings now
released from their confinement below ; distributing to them
their morning meal of " farinha," and their allowance of
water, rather more than half a pint to each, which they
grasped with inconceivable eagerness, some bending their
knees to the deck, to avoid the risk of losing any of the
liquid by unsteady footing, their throats, doubtless, parched
to the utmost with crying and yelling through the night.

A heavy shower having freshened the air, in the evening
most of the negroes went below of their own accord, the
hatchways being left open to allow them air. But a short
time, however, had elapsed when they began tumultuously
to re-ascend, while persons above, afraid of their crowding
the deck too much, repelled them, and they were trampled
back, screaming and writhing, in a confused mass. The
hatch was about to be forced down on them, and, had not

the lieutenant in charge left positive orders to the contrary, the catastrophe of last night would have been re-enacted. Antonio, whom I called at this juncture, turned away with a gesture of horror, saying, " No soy capaz de matarlos como anoche." On explaining to him, however, that it was desired he would dispose in proper places those who came on deck, he set himself to the task with great alacrity. As they climbed nimbly up, he made me feel their skins, which had been wetted by the rain : " Estan frescos,"—" they are cool."—" No tienen calor, tienen miedo." It was not heat, but fear, which now made them rush to escape from the hold ; and he showed me, with much satisfaction, how soon and quietly they were arranged out of the way of the ropes, covered with long rugs provided for the purpose. " Mañana no ha de morir ninguno :—acaso algunos de los que estan ahora enfermos."—" To-morrow there will not be one dead : —perhaps some of those who are now sick."

April 14th (Good Friday).—But one dead this morning. There are three in a dying state of the number trampled on the first night ; one, a robust lad, so dreadfully bruised and swoln as to be unable to move a limb, nor can we open his eyelids. An orange squeezed into his mouth, from time to time, seemed to refresh him. I observed two women creep out of the boiler in which beans are cooked for the negroes. On the first night, the females appear to have gone quietly, at an early hour, to a berth partitioned off for them between the rest of the hold and our cabin : it being the custom of slave-traders to keep the sexes strictly separate. At two, this afternoon, a large ship was reported to leeward ; soon ascertained to be the " Cleopatra," standing out from Quilimane, where she had touched on her way to the Cape.

April 15th (Easter Even).—The world can present no more shocking spectacle of human wretchedness than is contained in this vessel. It seems that a scene so harrowing can hardly be witnessed without an injurious effect on the beholder; its tendency being, first to overwhelm, afterwards, by familiarising, in some degree to deaden, the feelings. Perhaps it but reveals that apathy to the sufferings of others which the heart would be unwilling to acknowledge of itself. Antonio came to report to me that not one had died during the last night; adding, "Bien arreglados, no mueren."

April 16th (Easter Day).—The "Cleopatra" being within two miles of us, at daybreak, wishing to communicate, we bore up close to her, and, at 10, A.M., I accompanied the lieutenant on board. In a quarter of an hour we returned, bringing an old Portuguese, named Valerian, to assist in repairing our sails, which were old and weak; and a more important, as well as agreeable addition to our company, in the assistant-surgeon of the frigate, who proceeded to an examination of the sick. The majority of cases were those of dysentery and ulcerated wounds. One man has deep sloughing ulcers, from a flogging. "He cannot be worth much," remarked a Spaniard, "since he came into our hands not only ironed, but flogged." A poor child, six or seven years of age, has lost nearly the whole of his great toe, from the insect "niguas," or "jiggers." Another has a severe wound in the leg, caused by a bite from one of his companions. Various impediments have prevented us from assembling to-day for Divine service. Our situation, indeed, appears as unfavourable as can well be imagined to the repose of the sabbath; and I am still more puzzled than formerly at a remark in the "Life of the Rev. John Newton," to the effect, that he had never enjoyed sweeter seasons of communion with his Maker than during his voyages to the coast of Africa for slaves.*

* Cape Town, June 24th.—The passage in Mr. Cecil's "Life of Newton," is as follows:—" I never knew sweeter or more frequent hours of Divine communion than on my two last voyages to Guinea, when I was either almost secluded from society on shipboard, or when on shore among the natives. I have wandered through the woods, reflecting on the goodness

Monday, April 17th.—Almost a calm. The "Cleopatra" sent boats this morning, and took on board fifty of the boys. The disease among them, which had the appearance of small-pox, proves to be a virulent kind of itch.

Tuesday, April 18th.—The wind continuing very light, we received a second visit from the "Cleopatra's" boats, and sent further provision for the boys above-mentioned, viz. two sacks of rice, one of millet-seed, and a quantity of Monte Video dried beef ; of which last article alone the "Progresso" carries store enough to support all the negroes for two months. There are, besides, six hundred sacks, containing about twenty-eight pounds each, of small beans ; a great many of an inferior rice, and of "farinha." Below the slave-deck are stowed twenty-two huge water-casks, averaging five or six hogsheads each. The length of one measured was six feet six inches. The cabin stores are profuse ; lockers filled with ale and porter : barrels of wine ; liqueurs of various sorts ; macaroni, vermicelli, tapioca of the finest kind ; cases of English pickles, each containing twelve jars ; boxes of cigars ; muscatel raisins, tamarinds, almonds, walnuts, &c. &c. The coops on deck are crammed with fowls and ducks, and there are eleven pigs. A breeze springing up in the afternoon, and gradually freshening, the

of the Lord to me. Many a time, upon these occasions, I have restored the beautiful lines of Propertius to the right owner ; lines full of *blasphemy* and *madness* when addressed to a creature, but full of comfort and propriety in the mouth of a believer : —

'Sic ego desertis possim bene vivere sylvis,
  Quo nullo humano sit via trita pede ;
Tu mihi curarum requies ; in nocte velatrâ
  Lumen, et in solis tu mihi turba locis.'"

The terms of censure applied to the above lines are surely severe. The sentiment they contain appears as innocent as beautiful :—

Thus in the sylvan deserts would I dwell,
  Where never human foot hath trod ; with thee,
A solace to my cares ; in darkness fell
  A light ; in solitude, society.

" Cleopatra" shot a-head of us, passing so near that we could exchange farewell signs with our friends on board, who seemed now to be parting company in good earnest.

Wednesday, April 19th.—Antonio gave me to-day an account of his escape off Quilimane, and subsequent capture, on our second chase. The slavers supposed the " Cleopatra," lying at anchor, to be an American whaler. When unde-ceived on this point, and pursued by the frigate to the south, taking advantage of the darkness of the night, they hauled round, and, running back in an opposite direction, anchored between Quilimane and Fogo. Here they com-menced the embarkation of their cargo, which occupied ten days. " And had we not been detained," he added, " a day or two, waiting for provisions, we should have escaped you altogether. On the same night that we left the coast, we saw the lights of a ship, and tried to get out of her way, but there was little wind, and, at day-break, I mounted to the topmast-head, and—descubrimos la fragata." The negroes forming their cargo, are affirmed by the Spaniards to have been in a very sickly state—" mala esclavitud,"—when embarked ; having waited on the coast two or three months in expectation of a vessel. Some of them had come from far in the interior, and were received in wretched condition, and fifty were rejected as unfit to take. The vessel, they say, is capable of carrying five hundred, " bien arreglados y acomodados." Though little confidence may be due to the reports of slave-traders, I questioned them whether they considered the traffick likely to be abolished. Antonio, lifting his fore-finger to his eye, silently shook his head. Sebastian gave me his opinion that in Brazil, where many secluded creeks afforded facility for contraband ad-venture, there would be great difficulty in suppressing the trade, though the authority of the Government, if hearty in the cause, might do much. At Havana, he remarked, where for many years he had been engaged in it, and, at former periods, had seen twenty " negreros" lying in harbour at a time, and two or three go in or out during a day ; now, owing to the zealous efforts of the Governor, not one was seen to enter. At Quilimane, by his account, eight or nine vessels take in their cargo yearly, averaging, at the lowest, five hundred in each. " But now," he added, " none escape :"—" es una carrera de hombres perdidos :" —" it is a service of desperate men." Two vessels, as before mentioned, having been taken, and another driven ashore by the " Lily ;" the " Progresso" makes the fourth capture this year. One, however, they say, escaped a few weeks since from that coast ; and it may be doubted whether its profits will not compensate for the loss of the other four. On the east coast of Africa negroes are usually paid for in money, sometimes in " fazendas," coarse cottons, at a cost of about eighteen dollars for men, twelve for boys. At Rio Janeiro, their value may be estimated at 500 milreis, or £52. for men ; 400 milreis, or £41. 10s. for women ; 300 milreis, or £31. for boys. Thus, on a cargo of five hundred, at the mean price, the profit will exceed £19,000.

> Cost price of 500, at fifteen dollars, or £3. 5s. each   £ 1,625
> Selling price at Rio of 500, at £41. 10s. each .   . 20,750

" Es un comercio *terribile*," remarked Antonio. The epithet thus applied by him to the commerce, taken literally, though strictly appropriate, would be far from expressing his meaning, viz. that it is extremely lucrative. The pay of the crew in the " Progresso," as shewn by her papers, was at the rate of twenty-five milreis, about £2. 12s. per month ; to which, the Spaniards say, a present of five hundred milreis to each person would have been added on the issue of a successful voyage. They are both suffering under the coast-fever, against which, however, they bear up stoutly. Manoël, the Portuguese cook, on the contrary, gives way to it, has shaken hands with the sailors, and says that he is going to die.

Thursday, April 20th.—A negro died this morning from

having gorged himself with dry meal and crude beans. When thrown overboard, it being a dead calm, the body floated for upwards of half an hour, the face above water, close to the vessel, and sometimes striking against the side; while we were in apprehension every moment that a shark might approach and seize on it. Another negro suddenly fell on the deck, in violent convulsions; his eyes became fixed, his lips contracted, and we thought him dying. One of his companions, however, who speaks a little Portuguese, informed us that his fit was occasioned by having smoked a quantity of tobacco, wrapt in a piece of rag. After he had succeeded in swallowing a little water, he was immediately relieved, and lay down to sleep. A shed has been erected on deck, to shelter the sick, and another for the women, whose berth below is used for a store-room. The sick are frequently intruded on by others, who have no claim to be numbered among them, regardless of the injuries they occasion to the weak, helpless creatures whom they crowd and crush; the misery of their own circumstances, it may be supposed, leaving no room for commiseration of their fellow-sufferers. The great physical suffering of all seems to be a raging, unquenchable thirst . . . και εν τῳ ομοιῳ καθεισηκει το τε πλεον και ελισσον ποτον. They eagerly catch the drippings from the sails after a shower; apply their lips to the wet masts; and crawl to the coops to share the supply placed there for the fowls. I have remarked some of the sick licking the deck, when washed with salt water. Their dinner to-day consisted of four bags of beans, and two of rice, well boiled together, and affording a plentiful repast. It is distributed in tubs, round which they are seated, in parties of ten, and, at a signal, begin to dip their hands into the mess, and convey the contents to their mouths with great dexterity, but without any undue haste or greediness. Several of the younger boys have attached themselves to the after part of the deck, near our cabin, and will not leave the spot even during the night, having a piece of sail thrown over them. Their names are, Macarello, who appears not to be above six years of age, Quelinga, Carrèpa, and Catùla.

Sunday, April 23rd.—Squally weather, and a heavy sea, prevented any attempt at the performance of Divine service. To turn my thoughts from harassing subjects, I had recourse to a few books, hastily put into my bag, on quitting the ship ; and the first which came to my hand, a volume of Mr. Newman's Lectures, transported me at once to the spot where I spent this season two years since. On the afternoon of Easter Sunday, 1841, I heard their author preach, at St. Mary's, on the Passion of our Lord, and passed the evening of the same day, amid a kind and hospitable circle, around the fireside of Mr. Palmer, of Worcester College. " Keble's Christian Year," the constant companion, not of this only, but of all my wanderings in every quarter of the globe, affords a " treasure of sweet thought" in all scenes and circumstances.

> " Far, far away, the home-sick seaman's hoard,
>   Thy fragrant tokens live ;
> Like flower-leaves in a precious volume stored,
>   To comfort and relieve
> Some heart too weary of the restless world."
>   *Form of Prayer to be used at Sea.*

Tuesday, April 25th.—The poor wretch who has wonderfully lingered twelve days, since the contusions received on the first night, terminated his miseries to-day, and, when thrown overboard, sunk as lead. We are now just on the Tropic, having made only 350 miles on our voyage, owing to the frequent calms. The weather much resembles that which one meets on the Line, but little to be expected where we now are, at this season. "I saw a shark, sir," said a sailor to me this morning, " *twice as big as what you are*, swimming about the vessel." A large one was caught soon after, and, mixed with farinha, made a meal for the negroes, which they seemed to relish. We apprehended, on opening the monster, that we might find the remains of one of their late comrades, but the stomach was quite empty, which accounted for the ravenous manner in which the bait had been instantly seized. Half an hour after the entrails of this shark had been taken out, and its tail chopped off, both which operations it endured without a sign of sensation,—it was supposed, indeed, that we had drowned before bringing it on board,—on a bucket of salt water being soused on it, to wash off the blood, it began to flounder about the deck, and bite on all sides, as if in full vigour of life. This sight makes credible the stories which I had previously heard as exaggerations, of sharks caught and deprived of their entrails, on being thrown back into the sea, swimming off apparently as if nothing had happened to them.

Wednesday, April 26th.—Six of the English, including myself, are affected with feverish symptoms, though none in so severe a degree as the Spaniards. Manoël, the Portuguese cook, was reported delirious this morning, and unlikely to survive the day. I went forward to see him, in the men's hold, where he lay in a narrow crib.

" Camara de marineros," said Sebastian, " es como casa de los puercos."—" A sailor's berth is like a pig-sty."

" Como està Manoël ?" I inquired.

" Ah! Ave Maria Purísima! si escapa esta noche, no sè : es segun el Biscaino."—" He is like the Biscayan."

" And who was the Biscayan ?"

" Era un Biscaino, que venia con nosotros, que cayò enfermo, y dixò que iba à morir, y—en efeto murio."— " It was a Biscayan, who came with us, who fell sick, and said he was going to die, and—in fact he died." " Es estas calenturas de la costa de Africa," he continued, " es menester que no se acobardè ; que si uno se acobardè, en quatro dias muere."—" In these fevers of the coast of Africa, it is necessary not to turn coward ; for if one turns coward, in four days he dies."

The Portuguese could not recognise any one. To my question, if he knew me :—" Manoël, quem sou eu ?"—he replied :—

" Si, o tubaraŏ."—" Yes, *the shark;*"—thinking, perhaps, of the voracious jaws that were shortly to prey on him. At 2, P.M., he died. The body, sewn up in a hammock, with a shot to make it sink, was brought aft to the poop, where, the English and Spaniards attending, I read the Form of Burial Service appointed to be used at Sea : " committing his body to the deep, to be turned into corruption, looking for the resurrection of the body, when the sea shall give up her dead, and the life of the world to come." The increase of responsibility incurred by those who have been called to the high hope of the Christian, and the " greater condemnation which may arise from our misuse of the privilege, is His to pronounce, who will judge the secrets of all at the last day.

Friday, April 28th.—The outcries below in the middle of last night being greater than usual, I obtained a lantern, and having roused up the " Capitaŏ Pequenino," a boy advanced to the title of " Captain" for his serviceableness in speaking a few words of Portuguese, he told me the cause of the uproar. " Estaŏ roubando agoa." I descended on the slave-deck, with a Spaniard, and an English sailor, who caught seven of the ringleaders in the act of drawing water from the casks beneath. The long, loose planks which compose this deck have daily to be removed, to get at the water and provisions ; but the nightly depredators, in raising them, must at the same time displace a mass of living beings, piled on the top, regardless, no doubt, of any injury they may thus cause to them. The mischief resulting from their delinquency is, not the loss of the water abstracted, but the corruption of that which remains, by the foul rags which they dip into the casks to obtain it. The boys were anxious to exculpate themselves from sharing in the theft with the men ; crying, in their language, "Ouishi ouishi no capean,"—"the little ones do not steal." This morning the culprits were "seized up" with small cords to the fore-rigging, and received from fifteen to twenty lashes each from a rope's end ; a Spaniard, an Englishman, and a strong negro, relieving each other at the task. Six of the most able negroes have been appointed to assist in pulling at the ropes, and entitled "capitaõs marinheiros ;" distinguished by a canvas frock, with a daub of paint on the back, to mark the port and starboard watches. Their odd appearance and awkward efforts excite some mirth among the crew. "We ought to feel for the poor things," remarked a sailor to his comrade, "more than we do." "Ay," was the rejoinder, "but we do not feel for one another, let alone them." Even the more considerate seem prone to look on this unhappy race as an inferior order of beings ; as if the Almighty had not "made of one blood all nations of men on all the face of the earth." Thus one hears the expressions :—"*It* will die ;" "*that* is dying ;" "*that fellow* cannot live."

We have, at length, the luxury of a fair breeze, after a fortnight of calms or variable airs. Shoals of porpoises have been darting along on both sides of the vessel, skimming the water past us with surprising swiftness, or springing several feet through the air, and at every minute crossing our bows, where the sailors are bent, though vainly, on harpooning one of them.

Saturday, April 29th.—Last night I was awakened by the sound of taking in sails, amid peals of thunder, and lightnings the most vivid which I have anywhere witnessed. Flash succeeded flash with scarcely sensible intermission, blue, red, and of a still more dazzling white, which made the eye shrink, lighting up every object on deck as clearly as at midday. All the winds of heaven seemed let loose, as it blew alternately from every point of the compass. The screams of distress from the sick and weak in the hold mingled with the roar of the tempest. In the morning a strong gale came on, driving us back to the north. The heavy sea rendered it too dangerous to veer, and the vessel, from her extraordinary width of beam, being ill qualified to scud, we have lain-to since noon. From the rolling and creaking, one might fancy everything going asunder. The women's shed on deck has been washed down, and the planks which formed its roof falling in a heap, a woman was found dead under the ruins, killed, the assistant-surgeon supposes, by a blow, having no appearance of disease.

Sunday, April 30th.—The wind has moderated sooner than we had ventured to hope ; but the swell of the sea continues so high as to prevent our assembling for divine service. We are beginning again to make a little progress through the water in the right direction this evening.

Monday, May 1st.—" May-day," which, in *our* climate, brings on the sunny hours, in this hemisphere marks the approach of the cold. The naked negroes* begin already to shiver, and their teeth to chatter. This is a new infliction added to the former calamities to which this unhappy race is doomed.

'Ουκ ἔστιν οὐνδὲν δεινὸν . . .
ᾗς οὐκ ἂν ἄραιτ' ἄχθος . . .

If we meet bad weather on getting into colder latitudes near the Cape, as it is probable we may, increased misery and mortality must be the consequence.

Wednesday, May 3rd.—The gale has returned from the south-west, though with somewhat less violence than before. We are lying-to, under main and fore-trysails, the fore-staysail having been blown away. We feel the cold now severely. Seven negroes were found dead this morning,— among them a girl.

Thursday, May 4th.—The gale, which raged, like its predecessor, about twenty-four hours, has abated, and we have to-day light winds, apparently dying away into a calm.

* The females were distinguished by a cotton handkerchief around the waist.

Friday, May 5th.—The " Capitaõ Pequenino," who bears also the Portuguese name of " Luiz," came quietly to me this evening, and said, " Senhor, estaõ roubando aguardient eabaxo."—" They are stealing brandy below." I could not comprehend how this could be, as all the brandy in the hold had been started at the commencement of the voyage, to prevent mischief. Having reported it to the Lieutenant, I accompanied the two Spaniards to the slave-deck, and surprised a large party of the negroes, busily drawing up, by means of old rags, as usual, the contents of two barrels. One of these proved to be of water, and another smaller one, which Luiz supposed to be aguardiente, contained vinegar. Summary punishment was inflicted on eight, who were taken in the fact. They received by moonlight about eighteen lashes each, and were coupled in shackles previously to being sent back into the hold. Thus, as in many other fine beginnings, the end but ill corresponds with the " early promise." The sound of knocking off their irons, which thrilled so musically on the ear, when we boarded the prize, terminates in the clank of rivetting them on again, with the accompaniment of flogging. The result of their offence is certainly highly provoking, when, as is sometimes the case, instead of pure water, we draw up from the casks their putrid rags ; on the other hand, none can tell, save he who has tried, the pangs of thirst which may excite them in that heated hold, many of them fevered by mortal disease. Their daily allowance of water is about half a pint in the morning, and the same quantity in the evening, which is as much as can be afforded them.

Saturday, May 6th.—The two sheds built on deck for the females and for the sick, though an excellent provision during the hot weather, on our passing into cold latitudes, rendered their inmates more exposed than the rest, who took refuge below, till the weather, levelling both, put all on an equality. The shed for the sick has, however, been re-erected. Many of the negroes have letters cut on the breast or shoulder, which, Antonio tells me, are the marks of their respective owners, who, on the vessel's arrival at Rio, thus recognise their own property. An agent, "fattore," at Quilimane, in correspondence with the Rio merchants, having notice when a vessel is to be expected, holds the cargo ready for embarkation. The condition of the negro, he added, is much worse at Rio, where he goes forth ragged and wretched, "like a slave," than at Havana, where he is often better dressed than many of the whites.

Sunday, May 7th.—My congregation to-day consisted of ten : three officers, five sailors, two boys.

Tuesday, May 9th.—A heavy squall last night from the west, and this morning a strong gale. We hove-to, as before. The first objects which met my eye on deck were three lying dead on it : a man, covered by a coil of rope, a grim and ghastly object; the poor little boy, with the "jiggers" in his foot, who had borne his sufferings with great patience ; and a young girl, whose eyes yesterday were both completely closed from inflammation of the head. Their lives had been for some time but a burden to them, and could not have been much prolonged, but were certainly shortened by the inclemency of the weather. On looking down the after-hatchway, I had several times thought that I perceived part of a body between two loose planks, half hidden by others lying on it, yet as often concluded it must be some bucket or small barrel ; but at last ascertained it to be the corpse of a woman, who came yesterday to complain of her bowels. She was healthy-looking, well-formed, and in the prime of womanhood, apparently about 18. The weather last night having driven all below who could move themselves thither, she was in all probability killed by falling down the hatchway —a raised cover, called the "companion," having increased the fall to about six feet. In consequence of this, a plank has been placed mid-way down, to facilitate the descent. The wind is evidently abating this evening. Our gales, if formidable, have hitherto been, happily, of brief duration.

Thursday, May 11*th.*—I was called on deck soon after six this morning, to look at " the most splendid sun-rise ever seen. The whole sky was hung with parallel layers of cloud, not dense enough to prevent the beams of the sun from gradually piercing and tinging the entire mass with a bright flame colour. In the east, this was of a deeper hue, varied with rich green and yellow lines ; and, presently, the sun himself arose, fiery red, from the wave. Though a fine, it was certainly a threatening dawn, and gave omen of a troubled day. Clouds were rising from all quarters of the horizon, and the breeze, which had been fair and steady, gradually freshened to nine knots. At noon there was all hurry to take in sail, and at 2, P.M., we were lying-to under a gale heavier than any of the preceding ones. Had we shipped a sea, or lost either of our remaining sails, as we had now no spare ones left to replace them, our danger would have been imminent. Towards evening, we were gratified by the report of the helmsman, that " the heart of the gale was broke." A yellow haze however overspread the setting sun, and it continued to blow as wildly as ever. Squalls, rapidly succeeding each other, mingled sea and air in one sheet of spray, blinding the eyes of the helmsman. Waves, towering high above us, tossing up the foam from their crests towards the sky, threatened to engulf the vessel at every moment. The vessel, however, bending alternately each gunwale to the sea as it passed, then plunging deeply forward, but recovering herself with a bound, rode gallantly through the assaults of the winds and the waves.

Friday, May 12*th.*—I have to-day witnessed a spectacle such as I had frequently heard to have occurred in slave-vessels, but hardly know how to describe. In a tub, placed on the slave-deck, for necessary purposes, a boy was found, who had fallen backward, and, too weak to extricate himself, was smothered in it. He appeared quite dead ; but, on some water being thrown over him, showed some symptoms of returning life, though only for a few hours.

Monday, May 15*th.*—When the squalls, breaking heavily on the vessel cause her to heel over, and the negroes to tumble against one another in the hold, the shrieks of the sufferers, through the gloom of the night, rising above the noise of the winds and waves, seems, of all horrors in this unhappy vessel, the saddest. I went on deck in the early part of the morning watch. The horizon looks clear to windward, the moon just dipping into it, and day breaking in the opposite quarter. The first actor on the scene is Cato, our mulatto cook, bustling, in the imperfect light, among his pans and kettles, making a fire in the galley to prepare our breakfast. What comes next? The same dismal, oft-repeated tale ; three bodies, a man and two boys, lifted on deck from the hold. The man was one who had been savagely beaten by two of his fellows in misery three or four days ago. That the greater number of those who die have their deaths hastened by others overlying or otherwise injuring them below, is obvious from the fact, that they are found dead in the morning ; very rarely, at least, during the day-time. · It not unfrequently happens, that they are crushed between the loose planks of the slave-deck, affording space for their limbs to slip down beyond their strength to extricate. · The Spaniards, whom I found engaged in cleaning this deck, amid a scene of filth sickening to every sense, mentioned to me that, among the medicinal stores provided for the negroes, there are three which would be found of great use to them : " Macela" (camomile,) " Raïz de Althea" (marsh-mallow root,) and " Gomma Arabica." Antonio argued, not unplausibly, that the manner of the negro's life in his own country, " Como los animales in el campo," so different from ours, rendered different remedies suitable. According to his theory, the bitter of a strong camomile decoction kills the worms in the stomach, and the mixture of the marsh-mallow and gum arabic soothes and strengthens the bowels. He is to give his medicine a trial.

Tuesday, May 16*th.*—To my sincere sorrow, the " Capitaŏ

Pequenino," and another little boy named Francisco, with the chief of the " Capitaŏs Marinheiros," and several others, were brought up this morning, charged by Sebastian with stealing water below. I could hardly credit it of the two boys, since I believe they might always have got water for asking, as they had made themselves useful, and been treated as favourites ; except it be that, literally, " stolen waters are sweet." There was no doubt of their delinquency, as they hung down their heads, and did not speak when I questioned them. Their punishment was such as rather to frighten than to hurt them. That of the other culprits, though not severe, was attended by melancholy circumstances. One was in an advanced stage of dysentery, of which the execution of the punishment elicited the most revolting proofs. It so happened, that as another was lashed to the grating of the fore-hatchway, writhing about, and screaming with all his force, " Lambooya, lambooya," —their cry for mercy, two dead bodies were lifted up out of the hold, scarce two yards distant. There is among the negroes a man named Cimäo, whose grotesque countenance and gestures make him regarded as a sort of buffoon. He has been appointed successor to the " Capitaŏ Marinheiro," degraded for his late theft. One gave him an old jacket, another a pair of trousers, to equip him for his office. Sebastian, who holds his qualifications cheaply, eyed the proceedings with apparent disdain ; and having, like a true-born Spaniard, a *refran* ready on every occasion, said :—

> " Este es el viage Orinoco,
> Quien no muere se vuelve loco :"

which, I suppose, may be loosely rendered thus :

> " This is the voyage to Luckinabad :
> They who don't die become mad."

Thursday, May 18th.—There is a natural good-breeding frequently to be remarked among the negroes, which one might little expect. They sometimes come aft, on seeing us first appear on deck in the morning, and bend the knee by way of salutation. Their manner of returning thanks for any little present of food or water, is by a stamp on the deck, and a scrape of the foot backwards, and they seldom fail, however weak, to make this acknowledgment, though it cost them an effort to rise for the purpose. The women make a curtsey, bowing their knees forwards so as nearly to touch the ground. In the partition of the small pieces of beef in their tubs of farinha, the most perfect fair-dealing is always observed. One of each little party takes the whole into his hands, and distributes two or three bits, as the number allows, to each, and, should there be any remainder after the division, pulls it into yet smaller pieces, and hands them round with equal impartiality. After a meal, they express general satisfaction by a clapping of hands; a mode also used by some among them of asking a favour, or begging pardon for a fault. I have collected a few words as a specimen of their language.

Numerals.

Massoro . . . Head.		1 . Bossy.
Masso . . . . Eye.		2 . Peedy.
Macootoo . . Ear.		3 . Dātoo.
Maroto . . . Finger.		4 . Nāhy.
Macoonuy . Nail.		5 . Shānoo.
Cocy . . . . Neck.		6 . Danhātoo.
Mimba . . . Belly.		7 . Shenōmy.
Mendo . . . Leg.		8 . Sairy.
Maniallo . . Foot.		9 . Femba.
Yboono . . Toe.		10 . Coomy.

Names of Men.	*Names of Women.*
Shematonga.	Berezida.
Condivenga.	Citānia.
Chapanduco.	Banzuvēry.
Zàkalý.	Mandilacota.

Friday, May 19*th.*—Bossey, the boatswain's mate, who was attacked by dysentery a few days since, and taken into

our cabin, died this morning at four.   The poor fellow had
possessed a considerable stock of humour, was a singer of
comic songs, and a great favourite of his shipmates.   Two
or three days ago he said, " he knew he should not get up
any more, and should make himself happy ;" meaning that
he would banish all thoughts tending to make him uncom-
fortable.   I could get him to converse but very little.   Once,
on asking if he understood parts of Psalms which I was
reading to him, he answered very earnestly, " Oh, yes !"
His last action, when we inquired if there was anything
that he wished done for him, was to raise his hands above
the bed-clothes, and turn them clasped upwards.   The
assistant-surgeon, on a post-mortem examination, found an
abscess covering nearly half of the liver.   At 1, P.M., I
committed his body to the deep, all the crew being able to
attend, with the exception of one, suffering from inflammation of the liver, whom we have taken into the berth in our
cabin, lately occupied by poor Bossey.

Saturday, May 20th.—We have, at length, a fair breeze,
the first for many days, and are going three or four knots,
being now near the spot we were on ten days ago.   Antonio
has been essaying the virtues of his mixture on the dysentery patients.*   I am not sanguine as to its efficacy, the

---

* The following is a nearly perfect list of the medicines provided for
the negroes, found on board the " Progresso" when taken by the
" Cleopatra" :—

Linseed.	8 lbs.	Columba	4 lbs.
Marsh-mallow root	6	Electuario Cathartico	4
Pearl Barley	0	Cream of Tartar	2
Camomile	6	Senna leaves	2
Tamarind pulp	6	Ointment of Cantharides	2
Basilicum	6	Rose Ointment	2
Epsom Salts	16	Gowlard's Ointment	2
Gum Arabic	5	Mustard	2
" Flor de Sabugueiro"	6	" Borrachinhas"	2
Pomegranate rind	5	Adhesive Plaister	1
Manna	4	Resinous Ointment	2

disease having, in most cases to which it is applied, taken too deep root. He points to their shrunk bowels, the skin wrinkled in folds, and asks : " Esos tienen barriga, o que tienen ? no tienen mas que el pecho." One or two, however, who were in a state of emaciation, have begun to look better, and he pledges himself for their recovery. Only those cases, he says, are beyond hope in which the disease has made such progress as is marked by blood redness of the mouth and gums,—a horrid symptom generally observed in the more advanced stages. " Esos moriran, los otros no." The ulcer cases have put on so hideous a form that I can now scarcely bear to look at them. These poor patients are, almost without exception, affected by dysentery also, of which they are certain to die, even if healed of their ulcers.

> " Quorum si quis, ut est, vitârat funera leti ;
> Visceribus tetris, et nigrâ proluvie alvi,
> Posteriùs tamen hunc tabes, letumque, manebat."

A boy, wasted to as mere a skeleton as it is possible to conceive a living being, died this afternoon while Antonio was administering to him his camomile mixture. He had made him sit up to drink it, when he dropped his head, fell forward, and died in that posture.

" Mel Rozado"	1½ lbs.	Calomel	8 oz.
" Especies Pectoraes"	5	Ipecacuanha	6
" Ditto Emolientes"	5	" Balsamo Catholico"	8
" Especies Antiscorbuticos"	4	Spirit of Ammonia	9
" Cascas de Remaas"	4	Peruvian Bark	6
" Almofaris de Bronse"	1	Camphor	6
Le Roy's Purgative	6 bott.	Sulphate of Quieine	4
Ditto Emetic	3	Laudanum	4
" Agoa Ingleza" (febrifuge)	1	Sugar of Lead	4
Chloride of Lime	1	Powdered Bluestone	4
Bark Wine	1	" White Vitriol"	4
Castor Oil	1	" Lombriguera"	4
Phials of Opodeldoc	4	" Pos de Joannes"	8
Tartar Emetic	8 oz.		

Sunday, May 21*st.*—Our breeze continues fair, though still light ; the sea smooth, and the weather fine. All our crew were able to assemble within hearing of Divine Service, raising my congregation to fifteen. As it was late before all had made themselves neat and ready for attendance, I read only the Morning Prayer and Litany, omitting the Communion Service ; although the full service would hardly have caused any impatience among hearers accustomed, in the " Cleopatra," to the unmutilated offices of the Church,

> Whatever gale the labouring vessel toss.

I stationed the " Capitaŏ Pequenino," who has crept into favour again, at the main hatchway, to sign into silence the negroes below, if any should show a disposition to be noisy. The few on deck, principally females, remained perfectly quiet. After the service, I wished to question the "little captain," as to the existence of any kind of religious worship among the African tribes, but could give him no notion of what I intended to ask. Antonio, who came to my assistance, told me it was needless, as he, who knew much of the African coast, could assure me that they had not the remotest idea of any religion. " No tienen Dios, ni Santo, . . . animales son, viven en covados, en el monte, como los lobos." " They have neither God nor Saint, . . . mere animals, they live in holes of the rocks, like wolves." The only appearance of superstition, he added, prevalent among the native tribes, is their " fetish." They hang anything they fancy about their persons, call it " fetish," and venerate it. I asked him if, at the Havana, where his occupation formerly lay, it was customary, previously to baptising the newly-imported slaves, to give them any religious instruction. " No les enseña nada," he replied, " antès del bautismo ; no es preciso enseñarles nada, para bautizar los." " They are taught nothing before baptism ; it is not necessary to teach them anything in order to baptise them."

Wednesday, May 24th.—The breeze light and variable during the day, has been, these two last nights, succeeded by a dead calm ; the mainsail being lowered, to save it from the wear occasioned by the roll of the vessel, the other sails flapping heavily against the mast. It is now that we suffer great annoyance from the floul air produced by so many pent-up sick and wretched creatures. At the outset of our voyage, it was comparatively trifling, and I suffered little inconvenience from venturing down on the slave-deck, to see what the matter was, when any extraordinary noise or outcries occurred. It is superfluous now to make this descent, in order to inhale its atmosphere, which pervades every part of the vessel, and in our after-cabin is almost intolerable. Gold lace and silver articles, though kept in drawers or japanned cases, have turned quite black, through this state of the air. In the middle of last night I left my great-coat and grass mat, which have, in sailor's phrase, done duty for a bed since I came on board, and went on deck to seek a little relief, but in vain. There was not a breath of wind : nothing in apparent motion in sea or air, or the heaven, except the huge albatross, with wings extending sixteen feet, wheeling round and round, sometimes sweeping so close as almost to touch the taffrail, on which I was seated. I returned below, and heaping the cover of a large tea-pot with tobacco,* ignited and blew away at it, till the poor sick man whom we have taken into our cabin, complained that I was " stifling" him. Disorder, I think, in every sense, is on the increase among the unhappy blacks. During the late fine weather, they have spent the sunny hours of the day on deck, but when below, their cries are incessant day and night. Thinned as their numbers are by death, there is no longer narrowness of room, but increasing sickness and misery make the survivors more hard and unfeeling, and they fight and bruise

---

* We found on board a large stock of Quilimane tobacco, with a quantity of reed and clay pipe-bowls, for the use of the negroes.

one another more than formerly. Little Catùla, the finest
among them, who received a bite in the leg about six weeks
since, getting continual blows and knocks, the wound has
now become a deep spreading ulcer. Another fine intelligent lad has been lately severely bitten in the head. Others
have the heel, the great toe, the ankle-joint, nearly bitten
through ; and worse injuries than these, too savage to men-
tion, have been inflicted. Madness, the distraction of despair, seems to possess them.

Several sail have been observed within these few days.
So long a time had previously passed without our seeing
any, that we seemed " all deserted on the main," except
by the albatrosses and Cape pigeons, which have constantly
attended us for upwards of a month past. The latter, a
pretty species of bird, much resembling the pigeon in head,
beak, and fan-tail, with white breast and mottled plumage,
swim, in flocks of from fifteen to twenty, close to the
vessel's side. There is land in sight this afternoon,—the
first since the commencement of our voyage,—supposed,
from our observation, to be Plettenburgh Bay, between
Algoa Bay and the Cape. Some of the negroes point at it
with looks of interest and curiosity, but the greater number of them sit huddled together on the deck, their heads
resting on their knees, apparently in perfect apathy to all
around ; and surely a more wretched looking set of objects
were never assembled.

Saturday, May 27th.—The bodies of three boys lay on
the lee gangway this morning, awaiting the assistant-
surgeon's selection of a subject for post-mortem examination. Antonio, pointing to one of them, made me observe
his tongue protruded from his mouth, and a slight wound
on the neck,—indications that he had been strangled. It
appeared to me, from an occasional movement of the head,
that he still lived. The Spaniard said that it was but the
motion of the vessel ; but, on looking more attentively for
some time exclaimed. " Vive, este vive,"—adding, " però

està para morir,"—" but he is at the point of death." Some foam presently issued from his mouth, the heaving of his breast became perceptible, and he continued to breathe between eight and nine hours.

Sunday, May 28th.—Cape Agulhas in sight this morning, ten miles distant. We are still about one hundred miles from the anchorage in Simon's Bay. Our weather continues beautifully fine, and promises a favourable conclusion to a troubled voyage. During the Afternoon Service, the gentle swell of the bright sea, the silence all around, contrasted to the noise and stir of other days, and the " soothing tendency" of the Service, combined to give a greater impression of peacefulness than I have hitherto felt on the passage. Might the voyage of life, after its storms and vicissitudes, end as brightly and peacefully !

Wednesday, May 31st.—It is remarkable that no death has occurred to-day, though, during the previous seven days, the fatal cases have averaged four per diem. The ancient " Capitaõ" of the " Marinheiros" who was flogged on the 16th inst. for stealing water, and has scarcely shown himself above deck since, during the warmth of noon crept up the main hatchway ; but so altered as scarcely to be recognised. From one of the plumpest and stoutest of the party, he appeared reduced to little more than a skeleton ; the shrunk and wrinkled skin hanging in loose folds over the regions of the bowels, and that " sign of despair," the horrid appearance of blood on the lips, which marks the fatal stage of dysentery.

> " Sudabant etiam fauces intrinsecus atro
> Sanguine, et ulceribus vocis via sæpta coibat."

Thursday, June 1st.—The unusually high number of eight were found dead this morning, and we can no longer venture, as before, to throw them into the sea, lest the waves should wash them on the inhabited shores of the Bay, which we entered last night. The first sight which greeted our eyes when the morning mist had cleared away, were ships lying in Simon's Bay, two or three miles distant. Three pendants were discovered, and others imagined. A frigate, with topmasts down, was pronounced to be the " Cleopatra ;" or, as termed in affectionate familiarity, the " Cleo." " But how is this ? She has fifteen ports on her broadside, where should have been only nine." Just then a fishing-boat, which we hailed, informed us that the " Cleopatra" had sailed, a few days before, for Port Natal. The frigate proved to be the " Isis," Captain Sir John Marshall, from Mauritius. The brig " Acorn" also lay at anchor, returned from cruising on the west coast of Africa. As soon as the " Progresso" anchored, we were visited by the health-officer, who immediately admitted us to pratique. My friend, Mr. Shea, superintendent of the Naval Hospital, also paid us a visit, and I descended with him, for the last time, to the slave-hold. Long accustomed as he has been to scenes of suffering, he was unable to endure a sight, " surpassing," he said, " all he could have conceived of human misery," and made a hasty retreat. One little girl, crying bitterly, was entangled between the planks, wanting strength to extricate her wasted limbs, till assistance was given her.

Total number of deaths during the Voyage.

April 13.	.	.	.	.	54		Brought up	. 75
14.	.	.	.	.	2	May 1.	.	.	. . 1
16.	.	.	.	.	1	2. .	.	. .	. 3
17.	.	.	.	.	3	3.	.	. .	. 7
18.	.	.	.	.	1	4.	.	.	. . 3
20.	.	.	.	.	1	7.	.	.	. . 3
22.	.	.	.	.	2	8.	.	.	. . 3
24.	.	.	.	.	4	9.	.	.	. . 4
25.	.	.	.	.	2	10. .	.	.	. 1
26.	.	.	.	.	1	13.	.	.	. . 3
28.	.	.	.	.	1	14.	.	.	. . 3
29.	.	.	.	.	1	15.	.	.	. . 3
30.	.	.	.	.	2	16.	.	.	. . 2
			Carried up	.	75		Carried up	. 111

	Brought up	. 111			Brought up	. 129
May 17.	. . . .	. 3	May	25.	. . . .	. 4
18.	. . . .	. 3		26.	. . . .	. 4
19.	. . . .	. 2		27.	. . . .	. 5
20.	. . . .	. 2		28.	. . . .	. 5
21.	. . . .	. 4		29.	. . . .	. 4
22.	. . . .	. 1		30.	. . . .	. 4
23.	. . . .	. 1	June	1.	. . . .	. 8
24.	. . . .	. 2				
	Carried up	. 129			In fifty days	. . 163

Friday, June 2nd.—Previously to setting out for the village of Wynberg, where I promised myself some repose of body and mind, I paid a visit to Sir John Marshall, on board the "Isis," who welcomed me with his usual kindness; and, on my passage back to the shore, I once more called on board the "Progresso." Fourteen corpses,—six having been added to the eight who died yesterday,—lay piled on deck, to be interred this afternoon on the beach. A hundred of the healthiest negroes were already landed at the pier, to proceed in waggons to Cape Town. Most of the "familiar faces" were gone. My poor little Macarello gave me a look of entreaty to be taken away, but he, who first attracted our attention by his sleek, healthy appearance, is now among the sick. Catùla, too, with his bad leg, looked downcast, as indeed he has always done ; and when I tried to cheer him, the tears ran down his cheek. I was not prepared for the feeling generally evinced by the negroes on coming into port, which is that of evident anxiety and apprehension. Whether it arise from their thinking less even of present ills than of " others which they know not of," or from some particular forebodings, I could not gather. The hundred above-mentioned received each, on landing, a good new warm jacket and trowsers, and were placed quite snugly and comfortably in open waggons ; and it was a great pleasure to see their circumstances so amended by

D

the transfer; yet it was more difficult than ever to get a cheerful look from any one of them. I subsequently overtook them, half-way on my drive to Wynberg, at " Farmer Peck's," a place of refreshment for travellers, well known to all who have any acquaintance with the Cape, and found them not more reconciled to the change in their situation. The women had each a new white blanket, in addition to an underdress. " Berezida," " Banzuvery," " Mandilacota," readily responded to their names, but showed little signs of pleasure on the occasion. Doubt and fear were predominant, and their countenances resembled those of condemned victims.

On my visit to Wynberg, in October last, it seemed to me almost a Paradise. The season is now changed to the winter of the southern hemisphere, and the leaves are falling around. There still remain, however, some roses, and the air is fragrant with the scent of mignonette ; and certainly no spot can be better calculated to afford that rest to which, after fifty days on board a slave-vessel, one has some claim.

Wynberg, near Cape Town, June 19th.—After the lapse of seventeen days from their leaving the vessel, I have this morning visited the negroes in the buildings prepared for their reception at Papendorf, near the sea-shore, about a mile from Cape Town, where they are well lodged, fed, and attended. All were landed from the " Progresso" on the 2nd and 3rd instant, in number 222, the remainder of 397, showing a mortality while on board of 175. Of the 50 sent in the " Cleopatra," one had died during the passage, and one after coming into harbour. On cleaning out the " Progresso," subsequently to landing the negroes, the body of a lad was found beneath the planks, in a state of decomposition. Part of a hand had been devoured, and an eye completely scooped out by rats. At the time of my arrival at Papendorf, a burial was taking place, attended by the negroes in procession,—the ninth which has occurred among them since their removal thither. Of 28 left at Simon's Bay, not being in a condition to bear removal, 14 have died to the present date. The sick are still numerous. It was pleasant to remark to-day, the more cheerful, assured look of the liberated negroes. Their impression at first had been that they were destined to be devoured by the white men, and they were reluctant to eat, fearing it was intended to fatten them for that doom. The attendants, some of whom are of their own nation, soon freed them from this apprehension.

Heretofore it has been the authorised practice to apprentice negroes brought to the Cape in prizes, as servants or farm-labourers, for terms of six or seven years, according to their age ; the indentures of such apprenticeships including various conditions favourable to the negro. One of these stipulates, that the person to whom he is bound " shall cause the said apprentice to be carefully instructed, and as speedily as possible, in the Christian religion, and to be taken, when sufficiently instructed, to be baptised ; and also shall permit and suffer and encourage the said apprentice to attend public worship . . . and, when he shall have been baptised, shall immediately cause notice thereof to be given to the collector of Her Majesty's customs at the Port of Cape Town, in order that the identity of such apprentice may at all times be known and distinguished."

In consequence of an Order in Council, dated January 4th, in the present year, notice has been recently issued by the local government, that negroes under twenty-one years are henceforth to be apprenticed as household servants only, or in trades requiring " peculiar art or skill ;" male negroes of twenty-one and upwards, for one year only, as farm servants ; females of twenty-one and upwards, for one year only, as household servants. It appears that there is little demand among the mechanical trades of the colony for such apprentices at the present time. The agricultural colonists complain that the period of one year, for which the adult is allotted to them, is too short to admit of their deriving adequate benefit from his services.

CONCLUDING REMARKS.

Wynberg, near Cape Town, September 3rd.

THE circumstances which I have witnessed attendant on the present practice of the slave-trade have led me more carefully to consider the chief obstacles which impede its abolition. And *first in order* of these, appears obviously the impunity permitted to those who engage in that traffic. So long as slave-traders, though taken in the actual perpetration of their crime, are free from all apprehension of penalty attached to it, we may look in vain for its suppression. To such persons no other restraint than fear of punishment can be of any weight. It was evident, in the case of the Spaniards on board the "Progresso," that their only shadow of apprehension was that of not meeting, if sent to Rio Janeiro, equal favour with their Portuguese and Brazilian shipmates. The old Portuguese sailor, whom the necessities of his family had induced to embark in a slave-vessel, desired nothing better than to be sent back to Rio. The other thirteen, Brazilians or Portuguese, who had preceded us to the Cape in the "Cleopatra," we learnt, on our arrival had already dispersed wherever it pleased them, there being no authority at the Cape to deal with them as criminals. The captain, whom they reported to have perished in the surf near Quilimane, but who was concealed among them, embarked for Rio, with four of his companions, in an English brig, having obtained money, as has been since discovered, from an English mercantile house in Cape Town. It is not to be presumed that his motives for concealing himself arose from any other fear than that of

inconvenient detention until the condemnation of the vessel
should take place.* Here, then, is the evil which first
claims a remedy in carrying into effect the spirit of existing enactments for the punishment of the slave-trader, so
that he may no longer with impunity make a mock of the
laws and treaties ratified by all the civilized nations of the
globe.

The motives to such a course derive, were it necessary,
increased weight from the consideration that the sufferings
and mortality of the negroes, connected with their trans-
port, are, by the measures at present pursued to check it, not
lessened, but aggravated. It is too manifest, that, under
circumstances similar to those which I have related, the
capture of the " prize" must be an event far more disas-
trous to the slave than to the slave-dealer. It cannot be
supposed that the accumulated calamities which ensued to
the hapless beings on board the " Progresso," on their
transfer to the protection of their liberators, could have
taken place had they continued in the hands of their pur-
chasers. As the latter have the highest interest which men
can have in the preservation of an extremely valuable
cargo ; so are they, of all men, most qualified for the task,
by experience of the system best calculated to provide for
their health and safety, and by concurrence of able hands,
in ample number, to carry that system into effect. In
these respects, the reverse may generally be asserted of those
who, on capture of the vessel by a ship of war, succeed to

---

* The captain of the " Defensivo," a second Brazilian slave-prize
taken by the " Cleopatra," off Quilimane, soon after her return to her
cruising-ground, and brought into Simon's Bay on the 29th ult. (without
negroes on board,) treated with the utmost ridicule the notion of his being
considered in Brazil an offender against the law : remarking that, after a
short stay at the Cape, he might probably return to Rio and take command of another slave-vessel. He had been an officer in the Brazilian
navy. The slave-trade is, I believe, in Brazil looked on rather as a
sphere for spirited and skilful adventure than as a discreditable line of
enterprise.

their charge. Those who know the naval service are aware that a cruiser, especially on a sickly station, can often but ill spare more hands to send away in a prize than are barely sufficient for their proper duties in working the vessel. The number thus sent away will be further liable to reduction by sickness, from the tainted, unhealthy atmosphere to which they are introduced, and other causes peculiar to the change of their situation. Thus, in the case of the " Progresso," every seaman was in his turn disabled by illness. It is also to be remembered, that the officer in command of the prize, on whose exertions and discretion the welfare of the rescued negroes mainly depends, is encompassed by professional difficulties of a very engrossing kind, increased, in many cases, by the novelty of an independent command, and the weakness of his crew, should sickness occur among them, in a vessel unproved as to her sea qualities, worse provided in naval stores than those to which he has been accustomed, and on a coast probably strange to him. It is not to be expected that any individual can, in addition to these causes of embarrassment, be equal, in the care of 500 helpless beings, to a burden usually divided among fifteen or twenty persons, well trained to the work, and employed in it day and night. The advantage of improved medical treatment offers less alleviation to the sufferings of the negroes than would be at first supposed. All that medical care and skill, adapted to European constitutions and maladies, could effect, was tried, as far as circumstances would admit their application, by our assistant-surgeon on the negroes of the " Progresso," without success, that I am aware of, in any one instance. On the other hand, the slave-dealers, in their selection and application of the large stores of medicines found on board the vessel, may be presumed to have been guided by some experience of their beneficial effects. In general, it is certain that the augmentation of sufferings, under the present system employed for the suppression of the slave-trade, is such as to present an additional motive for the adoption of a more efficient course, by taking some measures which may give force to the penal enactments against persons engaged in that traffic.* While we boast the name of Wilberforce, and the genius and eloquence which enabled him to arouse so general a zeal against the slave-trade ; while others are disputing with him the claim of being " the true annihilator of the slave-trade ;" that trade, so far from being annihilated, is at this very hour carried on under circumstances of greater atrocity than were known in his time, and the blood of the poor victims calls more loudly on us as the actual, though unintentional, aggravators of their miseries.

I may in conclusion remark, that even after taking this first necessary step, the root of the evil, slavery itself, would still remain deeper than any penal measures, however strictly enforced, can reach. It springs from the present debased, demoralized condition of the native African tribes. The prominent feature of social relation in many parts, is that of absolute slavery to their chiefs. The barter and exchange of slaves among them, is as frequent as, in Europe, that of dogs or horses. I have mentioned the case of a chief from the interior, at Quilimane, who, though in no way concerned in the exportation of slaves, offered, in my

---

* May 15, 1820.—The United States legislature made the slave-trade piracy, with penalty of death.

March 31, 1824.—Great Britain enacted, that any person concerned in the slave-trade from January 1, 1825, should, on conviction, " suffer death, as pirates, felons, and robbers ought to suffer." The penalty was subsequently altered to transportation.

Nov. 15, 1824.—The State of Buenos Ayres declared, that their citizens, trading in slaves, should be punished as pirates.

Nov. 23, 1826.—Brazil signed a convention with Great Britain, stipulating that the carrying on of the slave-trade after three years from that date, should be deemed and treated as piracy.

In 1841, Austria, Prussia, and Russia declared by treaty the slave-trade piracy.

In 1842, Portugal became a party to a similar treaty.

presence, four of his train to Azevedo, in barter for a paltry musical toy. Parents will sometimes bring even their own children for sale. The abominable traffic, engrafted on this " degenerate and degraded state," confirming and perpetuating its ills; the wholesale shipment of slaves to foreign lands, involving the multiplied hardships of their journey from the interior to the coast; abandonment in sickness, or destitution of food, should their stay there be prolonged ; exposure to aggravated sufferings and mortality after embarkation, even under the most favourable circumstances ; these form the catalogue of charges against the slave-trader. The predominance of slavery, however, in the barbarous countries with which he trades, existed previously to his traffic ; and, should it cease, would still remain. No other measure can reach this evil than the introduction among their savage tribes of the principles of civilisation and christianity, without which blessings their state would be but partially amended by the suppression of the slave-trade. It is, indeed, little in our power to speculate at what period so glorious an event may take place. We may however, from a retrospect of the means, blessed by the Almighty in times past to the conversion of the heathen, gather that they differed in no slight degree from any at present in operation for that end. Though in modern times the labours of individuals have produced partial and temporary benefits, and some, whose " record is on high," have bequeathed noble examples of zeal and devotedness, those labours have left on earth no permanent results, their very traces having passed away with the zeal and devotion which animated them. When the spirit which of old converted our own and all the other once barbarous nations of Europe to the faith of Christ shall again animate His church—the only instrument which has ever availed to raise a single nation from " darkness and the shadow of death"—Christianity will again gain ground on heathenism, as in former times. A branch of that Church, once planted and flourishing in our own colony, may soon extend her arms to the barbarous nations on each side of the adjacent channel, and gather the savage tribes of Madagascar and Mozambique under the banner of the Cross. There is no other that can ever triumph over Slavery.

Additional selected titles from the Black Classic Press list

50 Plus Essential References on the History of African People. Asa Hilliard. 1993. 24 pp. (paper $3.00, ISBN 933121-83-0). Hilliard's bibliography answers these questions: Who are the African people? Where did they come from? What happened to African people as they journeyed through time and made history in the process? What is the state of African people today? As an annotated bibliography, *50 Plus* identifies essential references for correcting distorted images of Africa and its people. Asa Hilliard is the Fuller E. Callaway Professor of Urban Education at Georgia State University. *50 Plus* is an excerpt of his collection of essays entitled *The Maroon Within Us.*

Hand Me My Griot Clothes. Peter J. Harris. 1993. 82 pp. (paper $8.95, ISBN 933121-78-4). In *Griot Clothes*, Peter Harris creates a memorable and mythic character— Junior Baby. Hip and cantankerous, Junior Baby calls on the reader to be an ear-witness to the past and present. Junior Baby is a commentator on the lives and culture of everyday Black people. Relating the ordinary, Junior Baby raises the consciousness of readers with a narrative worldview that links Black men of the 90's to traditional Black values. Peter Harris is the author of *Wherever Dreams Live*, a collection of folktales, and has published poetry in many magazines. He is the founding publisher and editor of *Genetic Dancers, The Magazine for and about The Artistry Within African/American Fathers.*

The Condition, Elevation, Emigration and Destiny of the Colored People of the United States. Martin R. Delany. 1852*, 1993. 215pp. (paper $11.95, ISBN 933121-42-3). Delany published this skillful argument against slavery and the subjugation of Black people at a time of intense conflict between pro-slavery and antislavery forces. To underscore the capacity of Blacks to live as equals, he recorded their achievements in business, agriculture, literature, the military and other professions.

Concluding that Blacks would never be allowed to coexist with whites, Delany completed his analysis by suggesting possible locations for Black emigration. The republication of *The Condition, Elevation, Emigration and Destiny* provides an opportunity to critically examine Delany's views as representative of early Black nationalist thinking.

Titles available after January 1994

Breeder and Other Stories. Eugenia Collier. 1994. 194 pp. (paper $11.95, ISBN 933121-79-2). Readers have enjoyed the short fiction of Eugenia Collier in journals and in collected works. *Breeder* is Ms. Collier's first published collection of short stories. It includes standards such as *Marigolds* as well as newer selections such as the title story, *Breeder.* This memorable collection is warm, impressive and ready to read. A native of Baltimore, Eugenia Collier is a teacher and writer. She has published essays on various aspects of African American literature in *Negro Digest/Black World, Phylon,* and *Obsidian.*

A Time of Terror. James Cameron. 1982*, 1993. 207 pp. (paper $14.95, ISBN 933121-44-X, cloth $22.00 ISBN 933121-45-8). Three young men were arrested. Two were lynched. The third, James Cameron, with a noose around his neck and an angry mob calling for his blood, was spared. This is his story, told 63 years later with anger, insight and reflection. Cameron provides readers with an important and seldom-told victim's narrative of a terrifying chapter of American history.

First Light: New and Selected Poems. E. Ethelbert Miller. 1994. 144 pp. (paper $9.95, ISBN 933121-81-4). A master of the light touch and the grand theme, Miller takes readers on a sojourn through American cities, war-torn villages, and caverns of the heart. In poems without borders, Miller communes with diverse peoples and gives voice to those silenced by poverty and oppression. His work screams for answers about the whys of this world and brings home universal feelings. Here, politics and personal experience share the same bed. E. Ethelbert Miller is director of the African American Resource Center at Howard University. He has authored four previous volumes: *Andromeda, Migrant Worker, Season of Hunger/Cry of Rain, and Where are the Love Poems for Dictators?*

Christianity, Islam and the Negro Race. Edward W. Blyden. 1887*, 1994. 441pp. (paper $14.95, ISBN 933121-41-5). When *Christianity, Islam and the Negro Race* was first published in 1887, very few Africans had written about Africa. As a careful observer of the conditions of Africans at home and abroad, Blyden offers an early African centered perspective on race, religion, and the development of Africa. Although many of Blyden's views were controversial during his time, he gained the respect of notable thinkers of different races and classes.

African Life and Customs. Edward W. Blyden. 1908*, 1994. 96 pp. ($8.95, ISBN 933121-43-1). This collection of articles examines the social and economic structure of African society at the turn of the century. Blyden was a scholar, diplomat, journalist, educator, and prolific writer. His work has been regarded as "the first important attempt at a sociological analysis of African society as a whole."

Restoring the Queen. Laini Mataka. 1994. 128 pp. (paper $8.95, ISBN 933121-80-6). This collection of poetry ranks among the best of Black Nationalist literary works. Laini Mataka is a mature poet who offers a repertoire of a Black woman's experience in America. Her poems display her sharp wit, sincere political consciousness, and her genuine love for Black people. She celebrates Black men with a critical, yet sensitive and loving eye. The real beauty and value of *Restoring the Queen* is that it echoes the hearts and souls of so many Black women and men, young and old.

The Maroon Within Us. Asa G. Hilliard, III. 1994. 220pp. (paper $14.95, ISBN 933121-84-9). Written to provide strategies for the collective development of Black people, Hilliard's fourteen essays address issues essential for socialization, self-determination and cultural identity. Within the context of "community socialization" Hilliard examines the economic, educational, spiritual and political aspects of the African

American reality. Hilliard's insight is fresh and ripe with solutions to many of the problems that affect Black people in America.

African Americans in Pennsylvania: A History And Guide. Charles L. Blockson, 1994. (paper $14.95, ISBN 933121-85-7.) This broad survey of known and not-so-known facts about African Americans in Pennsylvania finds its core in the author's two illuminating themes. Resistance set in motion by oppression, and the spirit of self-preservation, according to Blockson, inspired countless Black accomplishments. Blockson details people, places and events that have shaped Pennsylvania's history, and America's as well. Blockson is one of the foremost authorities on the history of African Americans in Pennsylvania and on the Underground Railroad. This volume also contains extensive notes on stations, conductors, and passengers of the Underground Railroad.

Early Negro Writing 1760-1837. Dorothy Porter. 1971*, 1994. 660 pp. (paper $16.95, ISBN 933121-59-8, cloth $40.00, ISBN 933121-60-1). As a librarian and later Curator Emerita of the Moorland Spingarn Research Center at Howard University, Dorothy Porter has served researchers and students for generations. In *Early Negro Writing* she has compiled a rare and indispensable collection of writings with literary, social and historical importance. Included are documents from mutual aid and fraternal organizations, arguments about immigration, narratives, poems, and essays .

*indicates first year published

Order these and other *B.C.P.* titles from your favorite bookseller, or directly from:

Black Classic Press
P.O. Box 13414
Baltimore, MD 21203
410-358-0980

Please add $2.00 postage for the first book ordered, $1.00 for the second, and .50 cents for each additional title.